Contents

Introduction

Not Just a Pretty Face

Is contemporary corporate design dull and full of compromise? Do designers and illustrators approach commercial projects in a different way to how they approach private ones? Is the work that designers do for themselves "better", more "free", more imaginative than the work they produce for their clients?

These were the sorts of questions that first inspired this book. It is a select compilation of personal, cultural and corporate projects from some of the world's leading young designers. In their own words the designers talk us through the joys and sorrows, pitfalls and crowning moments, learning curves and tricky client negotiations that are all part and parcel of their job. It also examines some of the main issues that confront designers in the realisation of their work and how they define, segregate, rationalise or integrate their corporate, cultural and private projects.

In terms of technology alone, the world of design has changed so dramatically in recent years that designers are constantly having to develop and adapt new working strategies in order to thrive. Computers dominate the nature of the designer's trade and staying abreast of technological innovation and learning to use new tools as they become available is a gargantuan task. Designers have a huge realm of media at their disposal, the potential of which is growing and changing by the hour. This means that the sort of questions facing graphic designers are no longer just along the lines of: "Should this typeface have serifs or not?" but rather: "What about extending this corporate identity with a website based on origami folding techniques and an animated film as a spin-off?" The pace at which the field is expanding and splitting into ever more disciplines is also extraordinary. And thanks to the Internet, getting work seen and getting access to the work of other designers has increased a thousand-fold and become almost frighteningly immediate.

Designers have to be constantly aware and awake; they provide us with the signposts to help navigate the jungle of modern consumer life. They are fulfilling one of the roles that artists traditionally fulfilled in the past; that of giving us visual aids to help us make sense of it all. But they are also reflecting the overall mental state of the consumer world; one that has increasingly sophisticated desires and choices and yet one that is increasingly jaded by a glut of choice.

All this is quite a burden to have to carry, especially when you have to look for work, come up with creative solutions and pay the rent at the same time. So designers seem to be developing ways of working that enable them to move and adapt rapidly in this constantly shifting environment. Certain key words come up again and again in relation to this, the most significant of which seems to be flexibility.

Flexibility, in relation to co-operation with clients, other designers, partners, employees or entire multi-disciplinary project teams; flexibility in terms of media skills; flexibility in terms of location; flexibility in terms of being able to jump between huge corporate commissions and tiny private projects; flexibility in terms of budget; flexibility in terms of team size and flexibility in terms of personal philosophy.

In order to be flexible, the working constellations that designers are now choosing to work in are paramount. We not only enter information networks through our computers, but creative ones too. Increasingly, designers are choosing to work alone or in small groups, thereby maintaining their creative individuality (in that they only have to answer to the clients, not the design dicta of their own corporation) and the very necessary need to be light, versatile and mobile; to be able to adapt rapidly to different tasks in whatever medium. The result seems to be a way of doing business that comprises networked creative cells capable of rapid splitting and hooking-up with others. Fons Hickmann M23, for example, has a core team of four individuals, which can quickly expand, with additional freelancers, to a staff of 14 or more on a project-defined basis.

There are no longer such rigid rules defining which particular creative disciplines a particular design studio will lay claim to either. Fulguro are three young industrial design graduates but that doesn't mean they can't branch out into designing visual identities, packaging, animated films, furniture and interior design as well. Designers such as Precursor have big-budget moving-image clients such as MTV and the UK's Channel 4, but that doesn't stop them putting just as much creative energy into a humble wedding invitation or a mural for their local bar.

Flexibility rules when it comes to company philosophy too. It is not about dogma or manifestoes or taking political stands, it is about being able to change easily and quickly when necessary. Adapting and surviving? Not really, it's more a case of adapting and thriving. Even the Australian company Rinzen, who seem to have found themselves the ideal democratic set-up with their "collaborative" studio, are the first to admit that when that model no longer serves its purpose then they wouldn't hesitate to consider another.

"We want to be completely flexible, so if we decided next year that having a big office and employing 20 people was the way to go, then we'd do that. We don't jump up and down and say 'this is how we are going to do things forever', it's just how we are doing it right now."

Rinzen appear to have no ideological problem with moving from a collective model to a larger company, "if the benefits are appropriate to the needs" and the end result leads to improved quality of life for the partners.

Clients too are requiring more flexible solutions to briefs. To be able to remain relevant for more than a few months classic design briefs, such as corporate identity designs, need to be versatile and expandable; built to grow rather than with built-in obsolescence. The traditional, rigidly defined CIs with logos, letter-heads and logotypes are becoming a thing of the past. Bob Shelvin, Head of New Media at Diesel, sees flexibility in terms of a "lack of boundaries", which allows a company even of Diesel's size to manoeuvre quickly and get a campaign out there, without the heavy machinery of a big corporation slowing it down.

This flexibility in working and co-operating, also goes hand-in-hand with a new and very public kind of creative freedom of expression. The designers featured here devote a significant amount of their working time to unpaid, personal projects where they allow their imaginations free rein. Instead of leaving this work in a drawer or on the office pinboard, however, they are publishing it on the Web, in books and in magazines, and even using it as a marketing tool. Private work has become public work in a new, very immediate kind of way. It is getting seen by, and inspiring other designers, and perhaps more significantly it is inspiring clients too.

The possibilities in design at the moment are really only limited by technology itself and the ability of the operators to keep pace with it and use it, or to make ever more creative connections with others who can. The boundaries that remain are those imposed by our own minds and conventions and by over-complicated bureaucracy.

This book is by no means to be taken as a definitive survey or a theoretical treatise on contemporary design practices – if only because that would make excruciatingly dull reading – it is intended more as an encouragement to both designers and their clients. The more these boundaries between corporate and private work blur, in a creative sense, the less reason there is for compromise. More than ever before, designers have the freedom to experiment and push their own creative potential. Further, the work featured here shows that, far from being dull and boring, corporate design can be adventurous, ground-breaking, radical and even daring. Designers should not be afraid of channelling more of what they are capable of producing into commercial work as many clients are far more open to aesthetic challenges than some designers seem to realise or even want to accept. The message is: Go for it!

ANISA SUTHAYALAI

LOCATION: New York, USA

PROFILE: "I gained a BFA in Graphic Design from Chulalongkorn University in Bangkok, Thailand (where I'm originally from) in 1995. I started working at Propaganda right after graduation and stayed there for three years. After that I went to Savannah College of Art and Design (Savannah, GA) and earned an MA in Graphic Design. Then, it was off to Chicago where I stayed at Segura Inc. for almost two years. For the past three-and-a-half years, I've been living in New York, working for Design MW and then 2x4. In addition, I do my own private work under the name of Default."

MISSION: "I joined 2x4 in May 2002, mainly because of 'differences' at a previous studio. Honestly, I didn't know anything about 2x4. My friend sent me a link to their website and said; 'You might like it there — they're all Asian'. Once I started, I saw that 2x4 has a real variety of challenging work and most of the projects are exciting...plus it's really close to my boyfriend's apartment."

CLIENTS: "I continue to do my freelance work alongside my job. I designed the identity of my mum's wine company, a website for my sister, and collaborated on a book with my boyfriend. Now I'm collecting work, building my portfolio, and trying to get the name out there. And because of the visa issue, I have to stay on staff for a while. Default is (for now) just me, but I'm slowly setting it up with my friend in Thailand and it's growing little by little."

VITRA SHOWROOM

CLIENT: Vitra, Switzerland

BRIEF: Devise a graphic language for the new Vitra furniture company showroom in New York.

CONCEPT: "Vitra is a European furniture company, but for the American market it can seem somewhat cold and inaccessible. So we beautified it and made it more friendly. It was a huge job and pretty much wide open. I just couldn't imagine what it would look like when it was done.

SOLUTION: "The solution was to make 'furniture blossoms' with beautiful flowers. The idea came from a flowery bag that I did and the client saying, 'that's cute'. The result was a friendly yet functional design. We reintroduced Vitra in an approachable way using a more recognisable language that had a kind of warming effect on the market."

LESSON: "Having fun silhouetting furniture to make collages. Developing, refining and finishing."

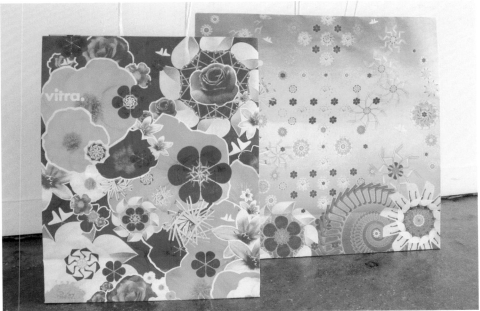

Cordiformis obconicus
Heart Cone Chair
Verner Panton, 1959

Mischobulbum cordifolium
Cone Chair
Verner Panton, 1958

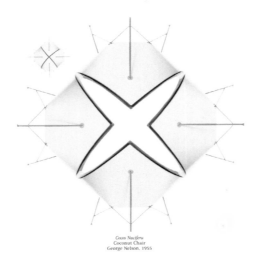

Cocos Nucifera
Coconut Chair
George Nelson, 1955

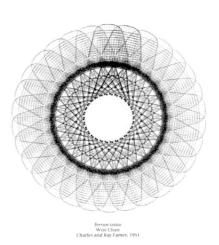

Ferrum textus
Wire Chair
Charles and Ray Eames, 1951

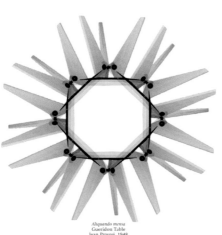

Aliquando mensa
Gueridon Table
Jean Prouvé, 1948

Oncidium papilio
Butterfly Stool
Sori Yanagi, 1956

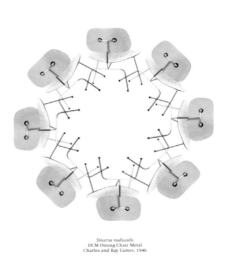

Sincerus nudicaulis
DCM Dining Chair Metal
Charles and Ray Eames, 1946

Floribunda inflicatus
Panton Chair
Verner Panton, 1967

Evidenter silva
DCW Dining Chair Wood
Charles and Ray Eames, 1945

FLINK

LOCATION: Antwerp, Belgium

PROFILE: In June 2003 Fanny Khoo and Tom Merckx joined the independent agency Bizart. The company changed its name and its approach and became Flink. "Our client services or products are often connected to a specific communication strategy that we've developed together. They are usually whole branding packages or communication systems. We concentrate on tackling larger projects that require a more conceptual approach, which is really satisfying as we are able to work in depth."

MISSION: "We don't have a predefined style or applied formulas, mainly because our clients come from many diverse businesses ranging from banking to confectionery. We are, however, very versatile in translating a new perspective for each and every project. It is important to not always do the design that the client wants, but instead do the one that they need."

CLIENTS: HRD (Diamond High Council, Antwerp), AWW (Antwerp Waterworks), AIB-Vinçotte and Akzo Nobel.

NEXUS CREATIVE PEOPLE

CLIENT: Nexus Creative People, Antwerp, Belgium

BRIEF: "We were initially asked to create a website for this special event and exhibition company, but they liked what they saw so much that they asked us to rework their visual identity."

CONCEPT: "The very first element created was a drawn branch, which was integrated into the rest of the branding."

SOLUTION: "We played around with the interchangeable design elements in order to create a combination of fluidity and harmony. The flower provoked this line of thought in terms of Zen and tranquillity. The NCP website was showcased on some of the best portal sites online. It created a lot of interest among creative people who wanted to be part of NCP."

LESSON: "As always, think outside the box. Also, finding a way to visualise NCP's abstract philosophy was a challenge."

Stan Colders
MEMBER OF NEXUS CREATIVE PEOPLE

Robby Magnien
MEMBER OF NEXUS CREATIVE PEOPLE

Michael Francken
MEMBER OF NEXUS CREATIVE PEOPLE

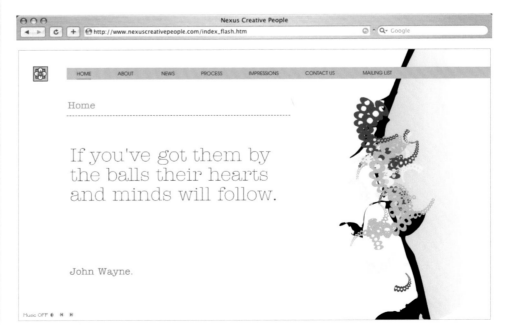

⊞ NEXUS CREATIVE PEOPLE

represents the best of creative
management, concepts and
business consulting.

Rather than specializing in one specific area, we prefer
to work across various media and with highly specialized
partners. This grounded approach means that we can meet
with our clients' diverse needs. This could be anything from
producing exclusive publications, a product launch to an
exhibition, etc. In addition to being a platform for creative
people, we find it equally important to maintain an ongoing
dialogue with our evolving network. These influences
stimulate us with refreshing ideas and inspire new projects.

Let us stretch your imagination and stir your thought processes.

NEXUS CREATIVE PEOPLE

New address

Lamorinièrestraat 127
2018 Antwerp, Belgium
Tel + 32 3 286.70.90
Fax + 32 3 286.70.99

New website

www.nexuscreativepeople.com

JUNG UND PFEFFER

LOCATION: Bremen, Germany + Amsterdam, The Netherlands

PROFILE: Eckhard Jung, a Professor at the Hochschule für Künste in Bremen and Florian Pfeffer, a graduate from the same art college set up a company together in 1998. Pfeffer runs the studio and teaches graphic design in Lebanon and Minneapolis. The studio now has eight members divided between the Amsterdam and Bremen offices.

MISSION: "We make other people rich – that's our philosophy. The target of our work is qualitative growth. The things we do are intended to provide people with real added value: economically, ecologically, socially, culturally and aesthetically. Communication design for me is a very personal issue", says Pfeffer, "I don't believe in the rule that says a designer should be invisible and step back behind his client's message or project. I believe in just the opposite; only if we bring our whole selves into our projects can we achieve valuable things. On the other hand, I don't believe in graphic design that refers only to itself and certain styles. For me that is just modern kitsch for visually-trained people."

CLIENTS: MTV UK, MTV Germany, Philips Eindhoven, Radio Bremen, Verlag Klett Cotta, Verlag Hermann Schmidt, Bundesministerium der Finanzen, Fraunhofer Institut für Medienkommunikation, Kieler Woche, Zanders Feinpapiere AG.

POETRY ON THE ROAD

CLIENT: Literaturforum, Bremen, Germany

BRIEF: "The brief was simple: the client wanted a book, flyers, a programme leaflet and a poster for the annual poetry festival, called 'Poetry on the Road', in Bremen."

CONCEPT: This was a collaborative project with Berlin-based designer and programmer Boris Müller. Pfeffer: "We wanted to come up with a solution that would not simply illustrate the event or superimpose an image on it. We wanted to create something that was equivalent to the event and also had a value in it's own right. We are fascinated by language and mathematics and we felt from the beginning that there was a lot to be gained from investigating and comparing structures of text and image that would allow us to create a system where text produces images, which would then form the identity of the festival."

SOLUTION: "We developed software with Boris Müller which transforms text into graphic images. We call this software 'Visual Poetry'. Each year we write a new piece of software (visual poetry 1.0, visual poetry 2.0, etc.) which creates different images from the poetic text."

LESSON: "We learned a lot of different things on this project. Firstly, never underestimate small projects. Through Poetry on the Road we got in touch with Radio Bremen who then commissioned us to come up with a complete redesign for their radio and TV station. On that project we collaborated with our dear friend Thomas Sabel who is now creative director of MTV Germany. MTV later commissioned us to create their new campaign for their off-air redesign. Secondly, always listen to your client (then do what you think is the right thing). Our first proposal for this project was rejected by the client. Then we had only 24 hours to come up with another solution which turned out to be the 'visual poetry' idea. The second idea was definitely better than the first. Thirdly, try to work with people you like, it is more fun and produces better results – thank you Boris."

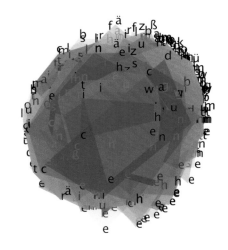

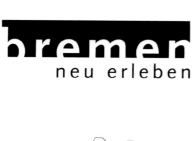

poetry ON THE ROAD

4. Internationales Literaturfestival Bremen
16.–19. Mai 2003

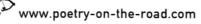

www.poetry-on-the-road.com

Fadhil Al-Azzawi, Irak/Deutschland | **Martin Amanshauser**, Österreich
Michael Augustin, Deutschland | **Elisabeth Borchers**, Deutschland | **Petr Borkovec**, Tschechien
Volker Braun, Deutschland | **Robert Creeley**, USA | **Frieda Hughes**, Großbritannien
Ursula Krechel, Deutschland | **Sosiawan Leak**, Indonesien | **Christian Lehnert**, Deutschland
Kgafela Oa Magogodi, Südafrika | **Michèle Métail**, Frankreich | **Ramsey Nasr**, Niederlande/Belgien
Hagar Peeters, Niederlande | **Klaus Reichert**, Deutschland
Jacques Roubaud, Frankreich | **Morten Søndergaard**, Dänemark/Italien
Yoko Tawada, Japan/Deutschland | **Peter Waterhouse**, Österreich | **Zhang Zao**, China/Deutschland

Schauspielhaus | Theater am Leibnizplatz | Schauburg
Kultourbahn | Paula Modersohn-Becker Museum | Institut Français | Kippenberg-Gymnasium

Programmheft und Karten bei: Buchladen im Ostertor, Fehrfeld 60, Tel. 0421/78528

Die Sparkasse **Bremen**
Kultur schaffend

literaturforum bremen : ● HOCHSCHULE BREMEN UNIVERSITY OF APPLIED SCIENCES **radiobremen** ⚲ Goethebund in Bremen e.V.

JORK ANDRE DIETER

LOCATION: New York, USA + Berlin, Germany

PROFILE: Dieter completed his diploma in visual communication at the UdK (Universitität der Künste), Berlin in 2003. While still at college he tutored the foundation course for Professor Ulrich Schwarz. He also co-founded the Berlin label Roomsafari and remained a member until 2003. Dieter places his intern experience on a par with his studies in terms of their importance as preparation for a life in design. "An internship with the fashion designers Utta Riechers-Wuttke and Martin Wuttke of NextGuruNow gave me an invaluable insight into the world of fashion, and time spent with Wolfgang Benz, founder of Werbewelt in Ludwigsburg, taught me how to be professional yet human."

MISSION: "I am a team player who works alone. I find visual communication solutions for a whole variety of client needs. I am a generalist, able to work on a broad range of projects. I get a kick out of finding solutions that work for both myself and my clients – nothing leaves my computer that I am not happy with."

CLIENTS: Breathe Cosmetics, Berlin; Gruner und Jahr, Hamburg; Ku'damm 101, Berlin; Süddeutsche Zeitung Magazin, Munich; Suite 212, Stuttgart; UCM Verlag, Salzburg; Yohji Yamamoto Group, Tokyo.

KU'DAMM 101 HOTEL

CLIENT: Ku'damm 101, Berlin

BRIEF: "Design invitation cards and flyers for the weekly '101 Lounge' events with live acts and DJs in a chic new Berlin designer hotel. The brief came from the Zurich-based firm Kessler and Kessler who developed the corporate design and CI for the hotel and are responsible for its creative direction. They asked for a lively and music-related adaptation of the hotel's logo – an apostrophe."

CONCEPT: "To use the corporate design guidelines in such a way that would appeal to the target group. The main theme behind the card series is movement. The motifs could also be interpreted as stills from a video clip."

SOLUTION: "I collected my ideas. I offered the best three ideas that I was happy with, that I would like to see in public, to the client. The results are two-colour (Pantone) cards that always refer back to the grey colour of the corporate design, combined with a fresh, seasonal colour. Additionally, the motifs reflect the calendar month; for example, spring fever in March."

LESSON: "Being able to take advantage of a very free and open brief while remaining true to the corporate identity."

Ku' Damm 101
BERLIN

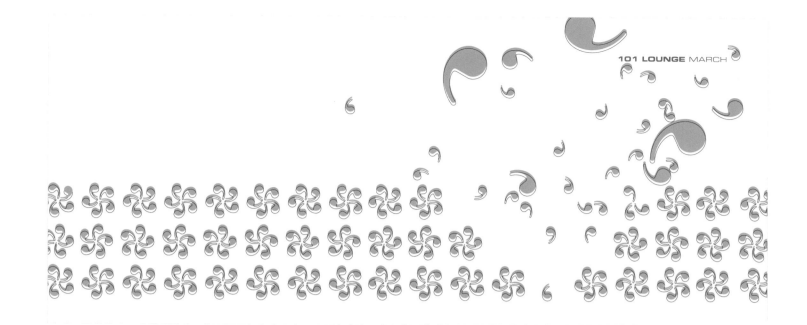

101 LOUNGE MARCH

101 LOUNGE FEBRUARY

101 LOUNGE JANUARY

PATRICK LINDSAY

LOCATION: Marseille, France

PROFILE: Lindsay is a typographer, illustrator, print and web designer. He took a two-year technical diploma (BTS) at Ensaama in Paris, which combined graphic design with commercial media studies. "The teachers at Ensaama seemed very traditional to us students; so out of touch with the 'new waves' of graphic design and the experimental work of the 1990s. We learned more from each other than from the professors. In 1990 graphic design books were rare, so we students shared our discoveries with each other, tried to emulate them, and then find our own way."

MISSION: "For me, making an image is a game. I work with a lot of intuition and pleasure; I am more of a craftsman that an intellectual. I work in illustration, graphic design, typography and animation, but I think they are all really the same. The titles 'illustrator' and 'graphic designer' are just terms for my clients and for my bills."

CLIENTS: Illustration: Le Monde Interactif, Liberation, Marseille l'Hebdo, Optimum, SVM Mac, Coming Up, Edition du détour (editor), Librio / J'ai lu (editor).
Print: Mairie de Marseille, Espace Culture de Marseille, Terre Active, Le Mur du Son, Calliope, Le Son du Mois.
Identity: Eye' DC, CCSTI/Agora of Sciences, Marseille.

EYE' DC

CLIENT: Eye' DC, Marseille, France

BRIEF: "'Do what you want and we'll see you later...', they said. I had to find a strong visual identity for my client that worked well in print, on the Web and with all the supporting media."

CONCEPT: "I did not have to create the declinations and variations of this project. The main difficulty was in creating a simple, graphic universe which could be used freely by other designers."

SOLUTION: "A decorative font built from the frame shapes of the company's glasses. I transformed the glasses into an abstracted pattern, removed from their original function and thus distance from the familiar object was created."

LESSON: "Learning to agree to see my work being used by other designers. In the end it was fun to see how these designers used the 'dingbats'."

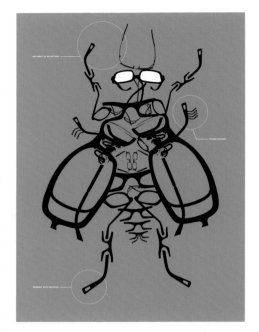

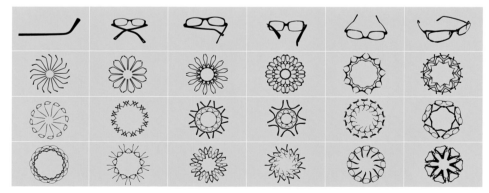

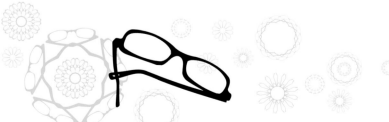

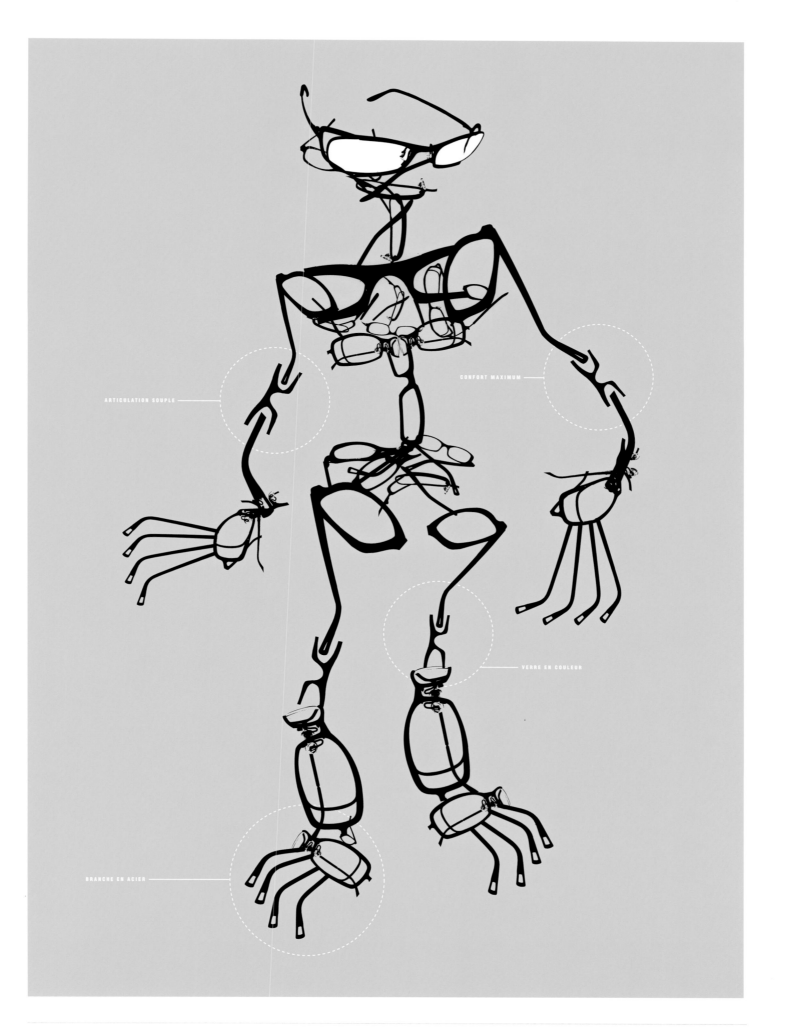

ARTICULATION SOUPLE

CONFORT MAXIMUM

VERRE EN COULEUR

BRANCHE EN ACIER

BASE

LOCATION: Brussels, Belgium

PROFILE: Base was formed in Belgium in 1993 by Dimitri Jeurissen, Thierry Brunfaut and Juliette Cavenaile. They quickly developed a design niche in the contemporary art world working with the likes of Joseph Kosuth and Malcolm Morley. They opened a second office in Barcelona (BaseBCN) in 1998 with a fourth partner, Marc Panero, which opened up a market in publishing and architecture. Geoffrey Cook joined the team and a third office followed in New York (BaseNYC) in 1999. Now Base has a staff of 32 designers from all over the world and a fourth "base" in Madrid.

MISSION: The range of Base's work is broad. While the studio retains graphic design as its core activity, Base is often called upon to develop comprehensive brand-image concepts and identity systems. Although about half of Base's work lies within the fashion and beauty industries, the studio also regularly takes on larger corporate, public and institutional projects. In 2001, the studio added BEople, "a magazine about a certain Belgium", to its roster. It is defined by the studio as a hobby which allows for freedom of creative expression.

CLIENTS: Corporate: MTV, The Surface Hotel, Cerruti hotels for SAS/Radisson, Milk Studios, Phaidon Publishing, Maarten van Severen furniture.
Fashion: PUMA, Wrangler Europe, Alexander McQueen Beauty, Yves Saint Laurent Beauty, System, Natan, Atsuro Tayama.
Cultural: MoMA, MoMA Retail, the European Convention, the Global Economic Forum, the Belgian Socialist Party, Cultural Ministry of the French Community, Steve McQueen, Bill Cosby Foundation, American Austrian Foundation.

BOZAR

CLIENT: Bozar, Brussels, Belgium

BRIEF: "Bozar" is the new name of the Centre for Fine Arts in Brussels. It is a phonetic amalgam of the Palais des Beaux-Arts and the Paleis voor Schone Kunsten that is intended to help both the French and Dutch communities, as well as foreign visitor, to recognise and pronounce the institution's name. Base was asked to develop an entirely new global identity around this new moniker. "The main problem was to maintain and express the prestige of the institution with a denomination that did not sound prestigious in either French or Dutch." A graphic system was required which would cover and unify all of Bozar's various areas of activity: art exhibitions, music (both modern and classical), cinema, dance, theatre, literature, etc."

CONCEPT: "The idea was simply to build the graphic system on the following; a composition grid; a headline typography using only Hoefler capital letters; splitting words and with all compositions starting at the top left hand side. The principle being that, it is not the logo that makes the Bozar identity unique, but its entire graphic system."

SOLUTION: This system provided the basis for the entire identity of the institution – a graphic signature. "This typographic system defines both the museum's locations (café, bookshop, etc.) and its activities (music, expos, theatre, etc.). It is also the house style of all its communication items (posters, annual publications, magazine, signage, etc.)."

LESSON: "We learned at an early stage that radical and clear-cut solutions such as this are often difficult for the client to accept as they are perceived to be too simple. It is only when one sees all of the applications developed as a whole that this type of system reveals its force."

BO ZAR EX PO

BO ZAR MU SIC

BO ZAR MAG AZ INE

BO ZAR MEM BER

BO ZAR CAFE

BO ZAR PU BLIC

BO ZAR ME DIA

BO ZAR COOL

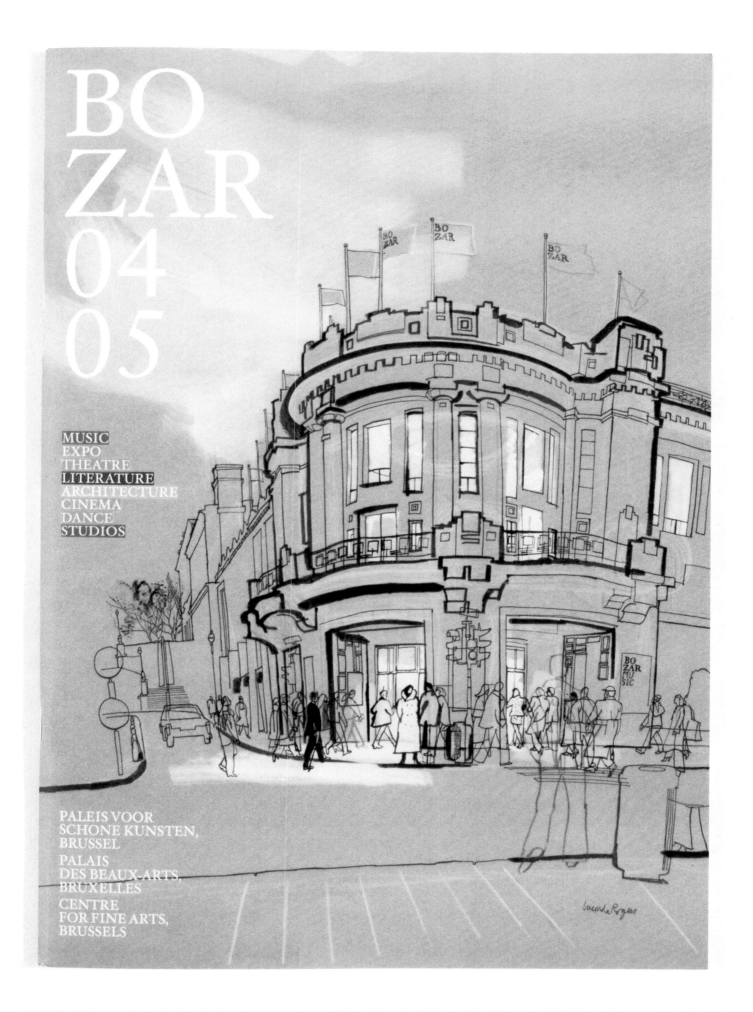

BO ZAR

04
05

MUSIC
EXPO
THEATRE
LITERATURE
ARCHITECTURE
CINEMA
DANCE
STUDIOS

PALEIS VOOR
SCHONE KUNSTEN,
BRUSSEL

PALAIS
DES BEAUX-ARTS,
BRUXELLES

CENTRE
FOR FINE ARTS,
BRUSSELS

Wrangler Europe

CLIENT: Wrangler Europe, Bornem, Belgium

BRIEF: To create and art direct the company's seasonal image. "The goal was to re-energise and rejuvenate the brand image, but a problem we encountered while working on the project was that our client wanted us to make the brand cooler, younger and more modern, but they were not willing to take any risks to achieve this goal."

CONCEPT: "The starting point was a list of adjectives defining the brand, such as open-mindedness, rough finish, etc. The tools and techniques we used and the applications we created had to express the following: freedom, liberation, low-cost and do-it-yourself."

SOLUTION: "It was done through the use of rough materials like tags, stencils, pieces of wood and tape and all kinds of 'deconstructed' and 'do-it-yourself' elements". The applications were wide-ranging; Base produced a fashion shoot; a booth for a fair; organised a large promotional event; shot films and designed all the various applications of the seasonal image. The "toolbox" that they developed was also used by all the external teams involved in the project: architects, stylists, video artwork and graphics, which resulted in "quite a strong global coherence".

LESSON: "The negative side of this project was related to the tremendously difficult working relationship with the Wrangler marketing team. They needed to be reassured constantly along the way. They asked us to be 'very creative' but actually wanted to play safe. Therefore every idea we proposed seemed to be a major problem for them to resolve. This apparent lack of confidence and uniformity of brand vision resulted in situations where we were almost adversaries. It was discouraging for us to feel that we were almost more motivated by the project than the Wrangler marketing team itself."

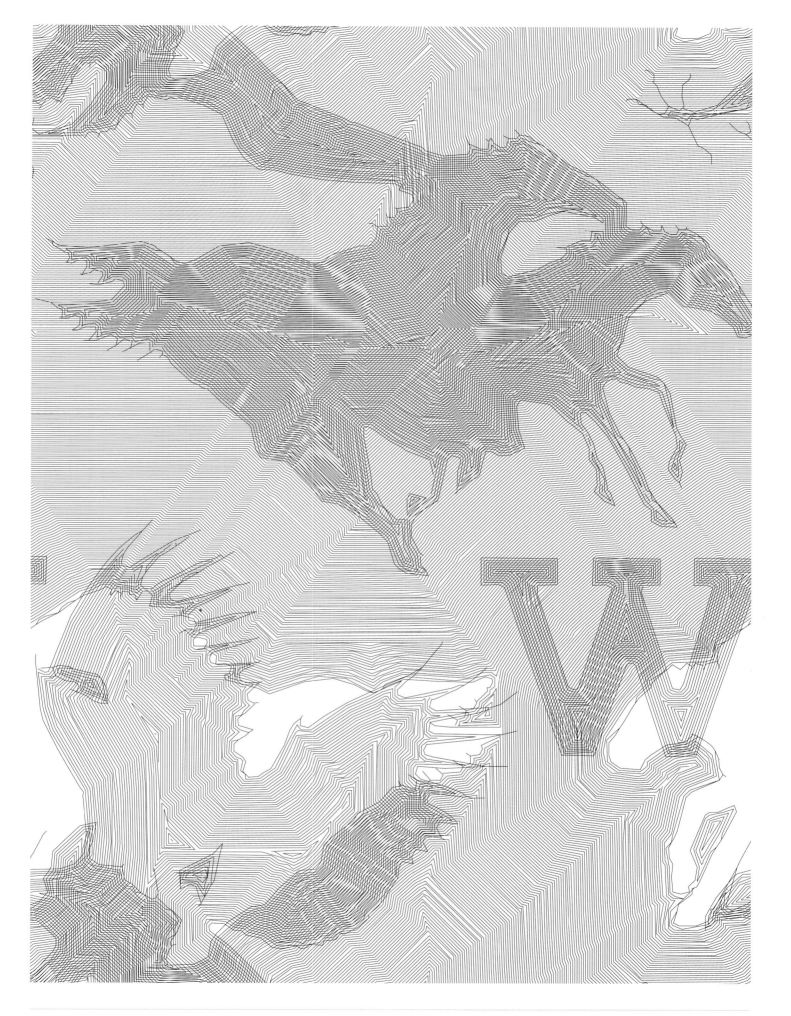

FONS HICKMANN
M23

LOCATION: Berlin, Germany

PROFILE: The studio was originally founded in 2001 by Gesine Grotrian-Steinweg, Simon Gallus and Fons Hickmann but, says Hickmann, varies a lot in size and scope. "There are ten of us at the moment, sometimes there are four of us, sometimes fourteen: Two graphic designers, one illustrator, one product designer, one architect, one carpenter, one historian, one advertising creative, one photographer and one musician." The staff all come from Austria, Germany or Switzerland. Hickmann himself is also a Professor at the University of Applied Arts in Vienna where he teaches, "Cognitive Dissonance, the Form Follows Failure Principle and Applied Football."

MISSION: "Aesthetics are regarded in a philosophical sense, communication in a social context and design in an experimental manner."

CLIENTS: Labor für Soziale und Ästhetische Entwicklung (Laboratories for Social and Aesthetic Development), Mercedes Benz Museum, Capital of Kiel, Diakonie, IFA Art Galleries.

YOUNG AND SOCIAL

CLIENT: Diakonie, Düsseldorf, Germany

BRIEF: To advertise a competition for ideas for social projects from socially-minded people.

CONCEPT: "Diakonie translates as: 'service to mankind'. Diakonie sees its duty as being to help people who cannot help themselves, in the Christian tradition of 'love thy neighbour'. Like other help organisations, Diakonie is not a non-profit-organisation, and is dependent on commercial success. It seems to be out of fashion to care about your fellow man. Western-style capitalism is in full bloom and ignores ethics. Nevertheless, Western culture is based upon social ideas and ideals. The aim of the 'social activities' of Diakonie is to enable one to confidently represent these ideals."

SOLUTION: "An innovative design for an old theme. We wanted to encourage young people to formulate social ideas and to put them into practice. We made posters and flyers aimed at teenagers and invited them to send in their social ideas."

LESSON: "Design can only be politically or socially relevant when it takes up a position and communicates content, everything else is just decoration."

DID001   DID002   DID003   DID004   DID005

DID001
3 NEUE ERSCHEINU
MEN 4 BERGERKIRC
DIAKONIE IN DER A
6 KOMMENTAR VOI
FRED KOCK 8 PORT
NATE UMMELMAN
ERSTE SPENDE 11 I
NICHT UNTER ACH
VERKAUFEN/SPIEL
VOM FREUND UND
HILFEN ZUR ERZIE
BIN ICH SÜCHTIG?
HAT IMMER EINE (
TE/DEUTSCHLAND
GEMACHT 16 ES GI
EIN LEBEN VOR DE
KURZMELDUNGEN
SUM 20 VERANSTA

DID002
2 SELIG 4 YOUNG AND
6 KOMMENTAR VON K
BRÜMMER 8 SONNTAC
ALS HERZENSSACHE 1
GEHT NOCH NACH DE
ZEIT 12 LEUCHTENDE
13 SPENDENWACHHEI
KUNFT EINES KINDES/
ATELIER 15 SOZIALE V
DER KIRCHE 16 WEGE
SACKGASSE/PUR/BET
IST EHRENSACHE 17 D
LITÄT? 19 URLAUB VO
20 ALLE AN DEN RUNI
21 PFARRER AUF KNOI
INTEGRATIVES KOCHE
KURZMELDUNGEN 23
24 VERANSTALTUNGE

DID003
2 UNGEFRAGT 4 G
VOM NETZ 6 KOMI
8 SUPPE UND THE
ESSEN, SPIELEN, L
LERNEN 12 SPEND
DAS SCHÖNE UND
HILFREICHE 15 YC
GOODBYE – WE SA
16 ALLE GEFÜHLE
GESPIELT 17 PETR
UND DIE DIAKONI
EINE KLEINE MAN
20 HAUPTSACHE I
21 DIAKONIE UND
GEMEINDE 22 KUI
DUNGEN 23 IMPRI
24 VERANSTALTU

DID004
2 FESTE FEIERN 4 FAMILI
SICH – DIAKONIE AUCH 6
VON WALBURGA BENNIN(
IN GOTTES WOHNZIMMER
TATSÄCHLICH 10 JUGENE
11 SECHS HALTESTELLEN
FORTSCHRITT 12 SPENDE
HEILEN HELFEN 13 FÜR E
UND GEGEN GEWALT/TRU
HORIZONT 14 AUS DEM S(
TRETEN 15 NOTEINGANG
16 SICHERHEIT PER KNOP
EHRENAMTLICH FÜR SCH
20 DIAKONIE UND KIRCHE
21 TREFFEN AM GOLDFIS(
SPECKSTEIN STATT SCHNA
DEUTSCHLAND GEGEN DI
ANSTURM AUF SERVICEW
23 MIT PINSEL UND SEGEI
RISCH ZUM ERSTEN JOB/I
24 VERANSTALTUNGEN

DID005
2 DIE QUELLE ALLER ZUKUNFT 4 DAS
HERZ SAGT RUSSISCH 6 KOMMENTAR
VON JOACHIM ERWIN 8 FÜR BANKIERS-
FRAUEN UND DROGENABHÄNGIGE
9 BARCELONA, ROM, PARIS, FLINGERN
10 BILLIG TANKEN IN FRANKEN 11 JUNG
UND SOZIAL: ES LOHNT SICH WIEDER
12 STERNTALER REGNETEN AUFS
TREBECAFÉ/TOM KANN JETZT WEITER
SCHWIMMEN/FÜR KINDER, ABHÄNGIGE
UND JUNGE MÜTTER 13 ALEXANDER
BLEIBT EINE LIBELLE 14 WENN DIE
MAFIA-FREUNDIN DOCH NICHT KOMMT
15 KEIN GELD FÜR VORSORGE/EHREN-
AMTSARBEIT VOR DEM AUS/DER KAMPF
UM JEDEN CENT 16 SPIELEN BIS MITTER-
NACHT 18 DREI, ZWEI, EINS – WEG FÜR
EINEN GUTEN ZWECK 20 SENIOREN IM
PROFIL 21 MENSCHENSKIND, KANN
KIRCHE FEIERN/ENDLICH LEBEN/KEINE
ANGST VOR DEM LEBEN IM ALTER 22
KURZMELDUNGEN 23 IMPRESSUM
24 VERANSTALTUNGEN

WEG MIT DEM MAULBEER-
BAUM: EIN WORT ZUR LAGE

FINANZEN BESCHÄFTIGEN. VORSTAND BLICKT
ABER ZUVERSICHTLICH IN DIE ZUKUNFT.

2 WORT ZUR LAGE 3
FINANZEN BESCHÄF-
TIGEN 4 SICHER IST
SICHER 5 MITARBEI-
TERVERTRETUNG
6 NEU IM DIENST/
JUBILARE/AUSGE-
SCHIEDEN 7 ES LÄUFT
UND LÄUFT UND
PADDELT/PRAXIS-
TAUGLICH/BRAND-
SCHUTZ: NEULINGE
GERINGFÜGIG VER-
SICHERT AUF DEM
RAD 8 MEINUNGEN

Design: Christof Nardin, Fons Hickmann, Simon Gallus, Caro Kornbrust
Editors: Thorsten Nolting, Christof Wand

DID MAGAZINE

CLIENT: Diakonie, Düsseldorf, Germany

BRIEF: To make a modern, up-to-date magazine for a conservative target group.

CONCEPT: "A magazine that communicates clearly and simply. No unnecessary details, no illustrations, reduced use of colour. We placed the list of contents on the cover. There is no theme, the title pages are always typographic and differ only in textual content. All photos in the magazine are by one photographer so that the typography and photography appear clear and straightforward."

SOLUTION: "DID Magazine is just one part of a complete new corporate design we did for Diakonie. It is a magazine for employees, sponsors and fund-raising. The whole emphasis of the design lies not just on the aesthetics but on content. On the back of every business card, letter and postcard is a quote from the Bible which could be taken as a thought for the day or as an encouragement to think of others first."

LESSON: Hickmann has been friends with and worked with Thorsten Nolting for nearly ten years. Nolting has been head of Diakonie for the last two years, but before that he was a vicar and founder of the Labor für Soziale und Ästhetische Entwicklung in Düsseldorf where he is very involved in the art, design and the electro scene. Hickmann found working together as designer and client to be a natural progression of their friendship, shared interests and differences. "Respect for each other's abilities allows us the freedom to make what one wants, and that leads to optimal results."

DIE QUELLE ALLER ZUKUNFT. DER GLAUBE ALS PERSPEKTIVE FÜR ALLE JUGENDLICHEN IN DÜSSELDORF.

„DENN DU BIST MEINE ZUVERSICHT, HERR, MEIN GOTT, MEINE HOFFNUNG VON MEINER JUGEND AN." PSALM 71,5

Für die einen steht die ganze Welt offen, die anderen bemühen sich, in Guinth Fuß zu fassen. Bei den einen fragen sich die Eltern, welches Hobby die persönliche Entwicklung ihres Kindes am meisten fördern würde, andere Eltern sind so sehr mit sich selbst beschäftigt, dass sie ihr Kind vor dem Fernseher vergessen. Wieder andere Eltern hoffen, dass ihr Kind nicht unter die Räder kommt in einer turbulenten Stadt, die sie selbst nicht verstehen. Jugend in Düsseldorf sieht sehr unterschiedlich aus.

Nach Jahrzehnten, wo alle Jugendlichen das Gefühl haben durften, sie hätten durch die guten Schulen, die engagierten Kirchen und die Sportvereine mit ihren Angeboten die Zukunft gepachtet, hat sich die Situation der jungen Menschen sehr stark differenziert. Und auch wenn die Kommune vieles versucht und die Diakonie und andere Wohlfahrtsverbände sich nach Kräften bemühen, die Chancen für alle so groß wie möglich zu halten, so ist doch zu spüren, wie Sprachprobleme von Zugewanderten, soziale Probleme durch Langzeitarbeitslosigkeit der Eltern oder deren hohe Verschuldung auf die Jugendlichen

durchschlagen als Verunsicherung, in Aggressionen und im Ausstieg durch Schulverweigerung. Nein, die Jugend ist nicht schlecht, nicht schlechter als zu anderen Zeiten. Doch haben wir darauf zu achten, ihre Situation zu verbessern.

FREIRÄUME SIND NÖTIG

Auf den nächsten Seiten wird dargestellt, wie wir uns für russlanddeutsche Jugendliche einsetzen und dass Freiräume nötig sind, damit eine Zukunft und damit Selbstbewusstsein möglich werden. Herr Oberbürgermeister Joachim Erwin betont in seinem Gastkommentar, wie wichtig es ist, niemanden die Perspektive zu nehmen und unseren Blick aufmerksam darauf zu richten, wie wir mehr Zukunft eröffnen können.

Nun ist Zukunft ein Geschenk Gottes, behauptet nicht nur der 71. Psalm. Dieses Geschenk brauchen besonders Jugendliche, denn sie tun sich schwer damit, sich von den unmittelbaren Problemen und der auf den konkreten nächsten Moment oder auf den morgigen Tag bezogenen Hoffnung zu lösen. Daraus erwächst manche Enttäuschung und Demotivierung. Auf Gott bezogen zu leben setzt eine heilsame Distanz zwischen das Heute und das Morgen und lässt daraus neue Möglichkeiten entstehen.

Wie ist das mit den russlanddeutschen Jugendlichen, deren fromme Großeltern unsere Kirchen bevölkern? Hilft ihnen dieser Glaube? Jugendliche richten sich an anderen aus, und da sie nur selten einen einheimischen Gleichaltrigen treffen, der den Glauben ihrer Kindheit teilt, da es eher cool ist, auf Kirche und Gott zu pfeifen, schließen sich viele dem an. In einer atheistischen Gesellschaft Glauben als Stütze zu erleben, das wird vielen aus den unterschiedlichen Ländern zugewanderten Jugendlichen schwer gemacht. Und auch hier gilt es, sie zu unterstützen, weil sonst für sie die Quelle aller Zukunft unzugänglich würde. Der Glaube ist eine zentrale Perspektive für alle Jugendlichen in Düsseldorf – denn aus ihm kommt Zuversicht und Energie für das Morgen.

THORSTEN NOLTING

FÜR BANKIERSFRAUEN UND DROGENABHÄNGIGE. NOTAUFNAHME FÜR FRAUEN KÜMMERT SICH UM ALLE.

Die Wohnung ist auf einmal weg, der Mann wird gewalttätig, das Leben auf der Straße ist nicht mehr auszuhalten – die Notsituationen, in denen Frauen stecken, können ganz unterschiedlich aussehen. Aber wie verschieden die Situationen und die Frauen auch sein mögen, seit dem 8. März gibt es für sie in Düsseldorf eine zentrale Anlaufstelle: die gemeinsame Notaufnahme von Stadt und Diakonie in der Querstraße 4. 365 Tage im Jahr ist die Anlaufstelle rund um die Uhr für Hilfe suchende Frauen da und unter Telefon 580 63 66 erreichbar.

Acht Frauen nutzten die Chance gleich am ersten Tag und waren sehr überrascht über den hohen Standard in dem Haus. Zu jedem Zimmer gehört ein eigenes kleines Bad, und wenn die Zimmer nur einzeln belegt sind wie in den ersten Tagen, dann fühlen sich die Frauen schon mal wie im Hotel. „Wir bieten hier aber keinen überflüssigen Luxus, sondern nötigen Schutzraum für die Frauen", sagt Heima Hesse-Lorenz, Sachgebietsleiterin der Diakonie in Düsseldorf. „Die Zimmer sind so beschaffen, dass wir auch Frauen helfen können, die in ihrer Not mit ihren Kindern vor unserer Tür stehen."

Die Erfahrungen der ersten Tage waren sehr positiv. Zwar saßen die Mitarbeiterinnen noch auf gepackten Kisten, alles sah noch ein bisschen kahl und nüchtern aus. „Aber wir haben ganz schnell gemerkt, wie positiv die Kooperation mit der Stadt und mit den anderen Anlaufstellen für Frauen ist. Die Vernetzung der Hilfen ist hier richtig fühlbar."

Bis zu zwei Wochen können Frauen in der Frauennotaufnahme Querstraße bleiben. Für eine längerfristige soziale und berufliche Rehabilitation gibt es weiterhin die Icklack mit sieben Wohngruppen für Frauen. Neben der Notaufnahme werden im Erdgeschoss der Querstraße auch die Büros der Fachberatungsstelle für Frauen und das Büro der Mitarbeiter für das Betreute Wohnen für Frauen ihren Platz finden. Bisher sind diese Stellen noch in der Langerstraße untergebracht.

CHRISTOPH WAND

BARCELONA, ROM, PARIS, FLINGERN. ALKOHOLFREIES CAFÉ DRRÜSCH IN DER CAFÉKULTUR EUROPAS.

Die Cafékultur in Barcelona, Rom und Paris kennt man. Die in Düsseldorf-Flingern ist neu – vor allem die der Diakonie. Trotzdem könne sich das café drrüsch in diese Kultur einreihen, sagte Wolfgang Heiliger, Geschäftsführer der Stiftung Wohlfahrtspflege NRW, bei der Eröffnung der alkoholfreien Begegnungsstätte der Diakonie in Düsseldorf.

Das Konzept des café drrüsch ist neu: Statt eines Rückzugs der Suchtkranken öffnet sich das café drrüsch in den Stadtteil hinein und schafft so Begegnung zwischen suchtkranken und anderen Menschen. Die Stiftung Wohlfahrtspflege und die Deutsche Behindertenhilfe – Aktion Mensch förderten den Umbau mit finanziellen Zuschüssen, weil das Konzept überzeugte, so Wolfgang Heiliger. Die Suchtkrankenhilfe der Diakonie in Düsseldorf gehöre zur Avantgarde ihres Fachs und das neue Café passe gut dazu.

Die Neugier war groß am Tag der offiziellen Eröffnung. Kolleginnen und Kollegen aus Diakonie, anderen Verbänden, Vertreter aus Politik und Verwaltung, Ehrenamtliche und viele Freunde drängten sich dicht an dicht im neuen Café. Bürgermeister in Marbes Smeets hob in ihrem Grußwort die Bereicherung hervor, die die Einrichtung zukünftig für die Menschen in Flingern und für die Suchtkranken bedeute – eine Bereicherung, die mittlerweile von fast allen so gesehen wird. Vor dem Umbau hatten einige Klienten Bedenken. Würden sie nicht zu sehr „ausgestellt"? Die Bedenken legten sich aber schnell, so Miriam Wied, Leiterin der Fachambulanz. Zu einladend sei der neue Raum – auch für Menschen von außen. Und gerade das sei Sinn und Zweck des café drrüsch: die Suchtkrankenhilfe aus der Anonymität zu holen und Integration und Kommunikation mit der Gesellschaft zu fördern.

KARL-HEINZ BRONCH

"In reality everything influences you, moulds you and changes your perception of things. The hardest thing of all then is to create your own language; unique and genuine, without obvious influences."
VASAVA

Part of the job of being a designer who's work is commissioned by and on show in the international commercial domain involves keeping "in touch" with, or even helping to define the Zeitgeist. Working at the cutting edge is often considered to be a brief and narrow phase in a designer's creative life, especially when it is linked to the world of fashion which tends to change "looks" every season.

Nille from Sweden: "If you aim to be a designer for a longer period of your life, you will have to face the fact that people fall in and out of love with your work all the time. But you will also discover along the way that there are as many audiences out there as there are ways to please them."

On the other hand, the jaded palate of today's consumer is becoming an increasingly difficult beast to please in many other areas of everyday consumption which means that "cutting edge" has come to sound more like a standard requirement in certain sections of the market. It is now not only possible, but wholly acceptable – and even encouraged – for designers to translate their own personal creative experiments into the commercial domain. Thus Lobo, for example, with their Lost Paradise project (see pages 176-7), can make an experimental animated film that ends up being part of an international TV advertising campaign for fashion giant Diesel. Or Martin Woodtli (see pages 44-5) can do a series of illustrations for a textile company's annual report that, by his own admission, do not illustrate the text at all.

That said, much corporate design, and design for institutions, requires a degree of adaptation on the part of the designer, even when the client has already taken the first step choosing them for a commission. Then it seems that the first priority for a designer is to deliver the desired result while maintaining their own integrity of style.

Lobo: "It's always a matter of finding a balance between our expectations and the client's. We may have more or less creative freedom depending on the project, but we always try to put out work that we are proud of and that meets the clients expectations."

Not separating commercial from non-commercial work can also be a useful strategy. Nille from Sweden: "I think one good rule of thumb is to try not to divide your assignments mentally into different categories. There shouldn't be work that you do for fun and work that you do for money. Turn the money projects into something fun and you will find that there is a lot of attention to be earned by putting effort into designing something in a field where people don't expect to find well-executed design."

Vasava too say they take the same approach to both profit and non-profit making projects. "The only difference is that when we work on our own projects, we know more about the objectives and let things mature by their own logic. When working with a client, it is they who set the rhythm. We have always considered that Vasava's first objective is not to make money, but to create good ideas."

This position, though, is sometimes only tenable in times when commissions are plentiful and there is the space for choice. What happens when "choice" becomes less of an option? Francois Chalet notes that so far he has not been forced to adapt himself too much to meet a client's wishes, and has been fortunate enough to allow his imagination free rein in his work; "Customers come to me because they want a 'Chalet' interpretation. The last few years have been very interesting because there was a lot of room for experimentation and taking risks. That has changed now. People have become more unsure, the [economic] crisis continues and now, more than ever, safety and the market are the main issues. It is hard to fit a "cutting edge" into such an environment. Nevertheless, I believe that there are still niches where something is possible."

Is creativity something that has to be nurtured and cosseted? Do designers and their office staff need to nip off for R & R weekends together in isolated farmhouses, to build twig wigwams and howl at the moon, to touch base with their inner selves? What about having special Zen spaces in the office loft filled with bean bags, humidifiers and surround-sound forest rainfall? Apparently not, for Kenzo Minami thinking outside the box is not something you can generate artificially; "You can't, just as no one can really think outside of their own universe – ever. You either just always do, or simply don't". For Sweden's Nille, creative thinking is not so much inherent, as about attitude; "The most important thing to remember is that anything you come up with can be used – anything". Precursor is equally down to earth when it comes to revealing the key to inspiration; "We approach projects in the same way as we have always done; with brains and sheets of paper, and it seems to work pretty well". Martin Woodtli also confirms that there is no magic formula when it comes to producing new and different work; "Good design simply takes a lot of time and energy. There is no technique that can do that for you. To allow your own attitude and interests to flow into your work

can perhaps mean that a job does not suffer and that you maintain your desire to do it".

It seems to be precisely because of this emotional involvement in the creative process – whatever the job – that many designers devote significant amounts of their time to personal, private, non-commissioned and often unpaid jobs. These can be as wide ranging as illustration work for themselves, musicians and other artist friends, charity work, publishing their own magazine, designing sets and furniture, making animated films, exploring new Web possibilities and collaborating with individuals in other media, fine art projects or creating political leaflets, posters and pirate Internet postings. Some, such as Fons Hickmann, go as far as to say that his studio works on a ratio of 50:50 no budget to commercial projects. Jonathan Barnbrook too says that half the work his office does is self-initiated, which means that they are not in the commercial world all the time. "We are very anti-corporate, anti-company here. People just lead their own lives and bring their own lives into the work. The thing that does help is doing personal work. We do things like exhibitions and our political work and that kind of strength of thought can then go into our commercial work."

This black and white division of doing commercial work to pay the bills and non-profit work for the benefit of the soul does not seem to be an issue generally. Instead, it's seen in terms of having creative outlets. Equal distribution of creative effort in a variety of projects is still emphasised. Nille from Sweden again; "As I said earlier, try not to divide your work into categories. The world doesn't need more crappy art-design projects. All the best designers I know of produce their best work under the pressure that a commercial assignment puts on you. Or to put it in another way; if you are really devoted to

something, of course you should do it, whether it is commercial or artistic (or both), but don't do it to balance your artistic ego. Nothing good will come out of it. Your commercial work will be dull and your artistic work pretentious and pointless. There are so many good artists in the world but so few good designers."

Vier5 even go as far as to say that non-commercial projects can be a downright pain in the neck; "Often, the low-budget and no-budget jobs are the worst. The people are constantly looking over your shoulder being annoying, constantly wanting to say their piece and discuss it with you and in the end you argue with each other. With no-budget, you usually need twice as much time and have three times as much hassle. The commercial client on the other hand trusts you, notices quite early on when he's in the way and leaves of his own accord and if he doesn't then you just push him out the door."

To reach their full potential, designers need to feel that they have a choice, to have a degree of control in what they create and for whom. For Ann Theobald from Surface, staying creative is not just about jumping in a linear fashion from one project to the next and trying to be "forever young and wild" is doomed to failure; "There has to be some kind of vision, some kind of way, some kind of strategy and you have to work on that".

But for many, such as Vier5, the preservation of creative integrity boils down to one deceptively simple maxim. "Only do work that you want to do and make sure that you are paid enough for it. That is the best and most elegant solution. Don't do anything that you don't want to do – whether it is paid or not."
The only difficult issue that remains is the task of finding out what you actually want and why.

JONATHAN BARNBROOK

LOCATION: London, UK

PROFILE: Jonathan Barnbrook graduated in 1990 after studying at St. Martins College and the Royal College of Art in London. He then established his own studio in London's Soho. "When I left college in 1990 I worked on my own for five years before taking on extra help. During college I worked as in intern at David Davies and Why Not Associates. Why Not was a good experience; they made me feel free in my work and really valued what I did. They made me feel confident enough for me to start on my own when I left college. David Davies was a very fashionable design company in the 1980s, and I was a little in awe of the place, but I don't think I really fitted in. It was good working with David Davies to see what I was not. I am far too intense, far too motivated by trying to change the world through design to work in a company that was just about doing 'nice' work."

MISSION: "I think that what we do is still pure and I think we do stuff that is original. Other people copy us; we don't copy other people. We are not prima donnas; design is about good communication on all levels, not just in the final piece of work. I think the individuality in our work comes from our serious intent, intelligence and the fact we have something to say – many don't. Our philosophy is; not to be too concerned about taking on jobs for money; to do the best work possible and to try and be careful who we work with. Also to try and do work that is experimental and to tell the truth. I think many people in design have forgotten these last two things."

CLIENTS: "Adbusters, Booth-Clibborn Editions, Mori Art Museum, Émigré and ourselves; about 40% of our work is self-generated such as staging personal exhibitions and designing our own fonts."

ROPPONGI HILLS

CLIENT: Roppongi Hills / Mori Arts Centre, Tokyo, Japan

BRIEF: Competition to design a new identity for the Roppongi Hills complex and subsequently to form the accompanying look for the Mori Arts Centre.

CONCEPT: "Because of the scale of the project, we were aware from the start that other designers would be using the identity. The idea was to create something that was flexible and open-ended. The literal meaning of the Japanese characters representing Roppongi Hills means 'six trees'. Six trees were found at the entrance to the building and six circular forms presented themselves in the word 'Roppongi'. For the Mori Arts Centre, to get away from the idea that art is purely visual; we created a series of logos based on the kind of waves found in scientific representations of light and sound. These waves represented different faculties of the centre and had to work both on their own and as part of a larger integrated identity."

SOLUTION: "We produced both identities and developed three new fonts in the process." Barnbrook then went on to do exhibition catalogues, packaging, banners, posters, leaflets and the design of the Mori website.

LESSON: "One of the most surprising and exciting aspects was the acceptance of our ideas by a large commercial group. Previous experience suggested that they would be conservative and have already formalised the approach they wanted. It is a credit to the people involved that from the start they were open and actively seeking an alternative approach. One of the most exciting aspects of the job was winning the pitch. We are a small studio and were up against many large and experienced corporate design companies. It was a great moment to have our radical and novel idea accepted...[which] challenged the predominantly modernist, 'one size fits all' approach to identity design."

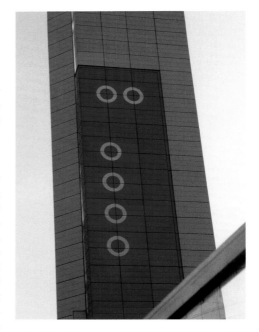

Photo: Jonathan Barnbrook

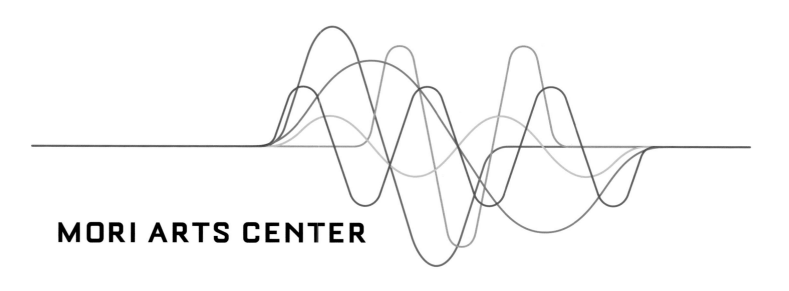

MORI ARTS CENTER

MORI ART MUSEUM
MORI ARTS CENTER

TOKYO SKY DECK
MORI ARTS CENTER

ROPPONGI HILLS CLUB
MORI ARTS CENTER

TOKYO CITY VIEW
MORI ARTS CENTER

MARKUS MOSTRÖM

LOCATION: Stockholm, Sweden

PROFILE: To keep up with all the clients knocking at his door Markus Moström started his own design studio, Markus Moström Design, in 1997 during the final year of his studies at Konstfack Universtity of Arts, Crafts and Design in Sweden. He works in areas that include architecture, graphic design and digital media. Other commissions range from packaging design, book design and commissions for cultural institutions as well as logotype designs and company profiles.

MISSION: Moström's design philosophy is to promote and maintain good ideas and a high artistic standard; to work with clarity and consistency; to have fun. He specialises in enabling companies to establish or strengthen their visual identity and graphic design. Of himself he says; "I'm an artist, but I never forget that I need to communicate through my clients".

CLIENTS: A3 Architects, Claesson Koivisto Rune Architects, E&Y, Tokyo; photographer Patrik Enquist, GG-Editorial Gustavo Gili, Barcelona, Haga Forum/Viljagruppen, National Guild of Master Painters, OFFECCT, Portuguese Chamber of Commerce, Stockholm; Ricordi& Sfera, Kyoto, SAS, SMI Swedish Furniture Industry Association, Svensk Form, The Swedish Society of Craft and Design Stockholm; the Swedish Institute, Stockholm; Totem Design Group, New York; Foreign Ministry, Sweden; artist Brian Wendleman, Stockholm; artist, Anne-Karin Furunes, Oslo; V&S Wine and Spirits.

SFERA

CLIENT: Ricordi and Sfera Company Limited, Kyoto, Japan

BRIEF: Create a new logotype/design profile for the company.

CONCEPT: "The idea was to design a logo that changes according to its application or location. To do something classic yet new; to do something that embraced both Western and Eastern culture."

SOLUTION: "To create a logo that is not a logo in the commonly accepted sense. We ended up being involved in everything from the logo to exhibition design. There was also close collaboration with the architects to integrate architecture and graphic design."

LESSON: "We mostly learned about the different ways of working, and how to communicate with a Japanese client. Working with another alphabet and symbols was quite a challenge."

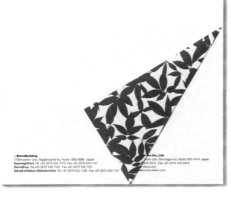

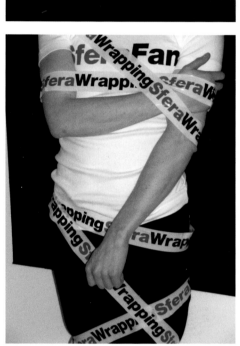

Nine Houses
Claesson Koivisto Rune

Publishing

No. 5 house

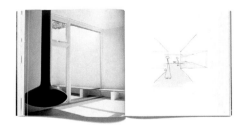

PIPPI-DAGEN

CLIENT: Astrid Lindgrens Barnsjukhus, Stockholm, Sweden

BRIEF: Design poster, invitations, ads and a programme for the anniversary and birthday celebrations of a children's hospital.

CONCEPT: Moström collaborated with Jonas Bergstrand on this project. "We wanted the resulting style and concept to be different each year. The event is for the children who are long-term patients; children with cancer and other kinds of serious illnesses. There are things you just can't do."

SOLUTION: "Every year there is almost the same content in terms of text and needs. To attract visitors to the party though, the idea has to change each time. Mainly it is about putting out information in an attractive way. The venue for the event is connected to a zoo, so animals are almost always a theme – funny and easy going."

LESSON: "To create different results, even though it is the same event and client each year, you need to learn how to forget about earlier solutions, find new energy and not be lazy."

KATJA GRETZINGER

LOCATION: Zurich, Switzerland + Berlin, Germany

PROFILE: Gretzinger, who sometimes works under the name of "Mikati" studied in Düsseldorf, Germany; "After finishing my studies in 1998 I moved to Zurich where I worked for Interbrand Zintzmeyer & Lux and TBS-Identity. In 2002 I started my own business with the redesign of the newsletter for the Rote Fabrik Zürich. I work alone or in teams depending on the project." Gretzinger is now in the process of establishing a second base in Berlin.

MISSION: "The main focus of my work is on typography and print media, magazines and poster design. I am also concerned with corporate image and company identity. Most of my work has conceptional leanings. I am interested in the dissolving of text into imagery; the form and the context that make a typeface a message before you have deciphered the signs. I work a lot with existing material or play with clichés. New content and interpretations are generated using distorted or twisted perspectives. I believe in the power of a simple design. A few elements put together in a particular way can say more things, more easily, than words can. The deciphering of these messages taxes the viewer and can be the message itself."

CLIENTS: Rote Fabrik Zürich, Funkstörung, Robin Minard, Zürich Jazz Orchestra, Moods Jazzclub, Monopol Magazin, Ernst Basler und Partner.

WASSERSTADT

CLIENT: (Project initiators) EAWAG (Eidgenössische Anstalt für Wasserversorgung, Abwasserreinigung und Gewässerschutz / Zurich Water Authority) and WWF (World Wildlife Fund).

BRIEF: "The original idea of the initiators was to design a project to mark the 'Year of Freshwater'. It should be situated in public spaces and deal with the theme of 'water' on a broad level. The main partners on the project were TBS-Identity, EAWAG and the WWF.

CONCEPT: "The idea was to break up the usual clichés. Therefore we didn't use the standard, shallow representation of water. The typographic and colour concept is a logical consequence of this idea."

SOLUTION: "In the end, we had almost 70 different themed posters distributed over eight different locations with flags, notice boards and installations as well as a website and a flyer."

LESSON: "Working together with eight different institutions was an interesting experience. A lot of individual initiative from the participants and the creative use of their own resources greatly enriched the project. Playful elements within an exhibition and the visual presentation of the contents are significant for the willingness of people to get involved with things. The quality of the content is often measured by the quality of the design. This was shown, for example, by the fact that most of the sponsors for the event were only finalised after most of the design elements had been visualised."

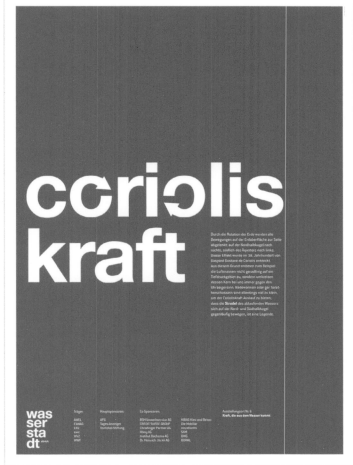

DAG HENNING BRANDSAETER

LOCATION: Amsterdam, The Netherlands

PROFILE: Brandsaeter is a graphic designer, born in Norway. He learned digital marketing and web production in the Oslo-based studio GEOX between 1999 and 2000 and then studied graphic design at Hyper Island School of Design in Sweden. He took an eight-month internship at Syrup Inc. in New York and graduated in Sweden in 2003. Brandsaeter currently works for QuA Associates, an interior, graphic and multimedia design studio, based in Amsterdam.

MISSION: "I think that, in general, my creative mission, is a more subconscious thing. For me its not something I keep in the back of my head, rather its something I cannot change. I believe my goal, is to push a project or a brief, no matter how isolated or stubborn the client is, so that I will be happy with the final results. I want to relate to and stand by whatever I create."

CLIENTS: Lee Jeans, M-Magazine, Hunter Gatherer, HUGA, NYC.

LEE JEANS

CLIENT: M-Magazine and Lee Jeans, Frankfurt, Germany

BRIEF: "Chester Reynolds created Buddy Lee in 1920-21 for the H.D.Lee Company as an advertising tool. I was asked to create an editorial spread, in a 1920s-style themed; 'Buddy Lee travelling the world'."

CONCEPT: "The idea was to follow Buddy throughout his journey and make a memory game of it, so we gathered together all sorts of old items and souvenirs that could indicate where he had been and what he had been up to."

SOLUTION: "The game is quite simple. Look at one page of the spread and remember the souvenirs, then turn to the next page to find which souvenirs are missing. This was made possible by adding a semi-transparent page in the middle that separated the two pages. I think the biggest challenge was that I wanted to create a 1920s environment, inspired by the great graphic design masters of that era and by creating something new, but without copying."

LESSON: "The communication between myself and Kimberly Lloyd, the editor of M-Magazine was very good, so we decided early on which route to take with the project. It was a reminder of how extremely important good communication with the client is. I don't believe that this project would ever have succeeded if Kimberly and myself had not got on so well."

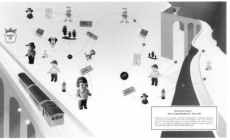

GROLSCH

CLIENT: Grolsch Music Café, Amsterdam, The Netherlands

BRIEF: "QuA Associates developed the concept and design for a new café/restaurant at the Arena Boulevard. The bar has an interior based on musical elements combined with a nautical atmosphere. I was asked to make site-specific graphics to be used inside the café, such as wallpaper and staff clothing."

CONCEPT: "The goal was to create something that would be a counterpoint to the sleek and elegant interior. The graphics would be there to create the mood and atmosphere we were looking for."

SOLUTION: "The graphics were based on the concept of Grolsch meets TMF (the music channel). I wanted to create something rich in colour and at the same time very stylish, sleek and elegant."

LESSON: "I've never really made graphics for an interior before, nor have I worked together with architects, but I think it is by far the most fun I've ever had on a project. I've learned how an image can be improved by using not just one medium, but by combining them."

PHANTOM:
RESEARCH
FOUNDATION

LOCATION: London, UK + New York, USA

PROFILE: The Phantom:researchfoundation is an artists', musicians' and designers' collective originally founded by Stephen Johnston and Michael Spoljaric sometime around 1999. Most of the time throughout their association Johnston and Spoljaric have been living in different cities, in different environments and on different continents and feel that this contributes significantly to the nature of their combined output. Johnston currently resides in London and Spoljaric in New York. Both partners have had long-term experience in developing projects for major brands across TV, print and advertising.

MISSION: Spoljaric and Johnston created the Phantom:researchfoundation as an environment in which to be playful and not take themselves too seriously. They believe that operating as a collective gives them total freedom and flexibility; when someone with a certain skill is required for a job, they bring them in to work with the team.

CLIENTS: Spontaneous, Social UK, Nike.

SPONTANEOUS

CLIENT: Spontaneous, New York, USA

BRIEF: A series of magazine adverts for an ideas company whose work spans a broad spectrum from design to live action, visual effects and animation. Phantom:researchfoundation were given around 50 images to work with that had been shot by Juan Delcan, the creative director of Spontaneous.

CONCEPT: Michael Spoljaric's concept was, "to be spontaneous without the clichés. At first we had loads of ideas for the adverts; naked people in Times Square, that kind of thing. But we were more excited by the idea of the viewer looking at the advert and not having the 'joke' come right out and smack them in the face. We wanted a grenade effect so you could look at it a few times and not get tired of the 'joke'."

SOLUTION: The resulting posters came from: "luck and a 'spontaneous' burst of goofing off on the machine".

LESSON: The best thing about the job for Spoljaric was, "getting it done with very few compromises. It is rare to work with a company that is full of good ideas and very encouraging".

ITF
GRAFIK DESIGN

LOCATION: Berlin, Hamburg, Stuttgart, Germany

PROFILE: ITF is a company of four individuals; Claudia Kahl, Till Sperrle, Tim Reuscher and Axel Pfaender. They met while studying graphic design at the Akedemie der Bildenden Künste Stuttgart and formed the company in 2003, after working together for six years in various constellations. They are based in three German cities and work together in various combinations for various projects, sometimes remixing each other's work.

MISSION: " ITF stands for 'In True Friendship'. The basis of ITF is the friendship that connects the four of us, and the great respect we have for each other's work. We enjoy working with people we like and on projects we can relate to. A lot of our projects are in the field of cultural production (architecture, music, publishing etc.). ITF has a great diversity of styles rather than one defined, corporate 'look'. We like to work as authors as well as designers. Our favourite projects are the ones that deal with society in a critical and reflective way. We really love detail and also humour is a major issue. We believe – like the designers of the Modernist avant-garde – that design actually has the power to change the world. This might sound naïve but at least it's a beautiful idea and a real motivation. Sometimes more is more: more passion, more humour, more love makes more impact."

CLIENTS: Superschool, Redaktion & Alltag, Galerie Neu, Bundeszentrale für politische Bildung, Dial Rec., Lautsprecher Verlag, the Beautiful Crew, Goethe Institute, Künstlerhaus Stuttgart, Starship, L'Age d'Or Music GmbH.

PRO QM

CLIENT: Pro Qm bookshop, Berlin, Germany

BRIEF: To create a corporate design representing the bookshop in printed and electronic media.

CONCEPT: "The goal was to create a very flexible corporate design that could be adapted to the challenging requirements of a newly founded enterprise with diverse and evolving activities. The visual appearance of the shop needed to reflect it's programme, which is focused on architecture, design and cultural politics, yet stay within a very limited budget. There was also a strong personal involvement since the clients are very good friends."

SOLUTION: A "look and feel" was developed, which included a logotype, a mascot / character, stationery and flyer templates that used various different elements. Applications such as ads and flyers regular expand the visual repertoire of the corporate design.

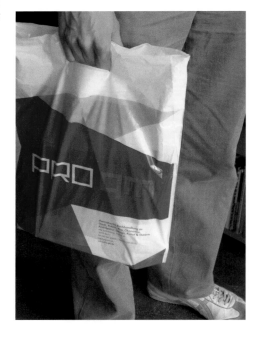

LAST SEASON
‹BÜCHER›

PRO qm

thematische Buchhandlung
zu Stadt, Politik, Pop,
Ökonomie, Architektur,
Design, Kunst & Theorie

La Biennale di Venezia: Less Aesthetics, More Ethics. General Katalogue AA London: Frederick Kiesler 1890-1965   Berke, Harris: Architecture of the Everyday   Hauptstadt Berlin. Internationaler Städtebaulicher Wettbewerb 1957/58   Biesele: Graphic Design International   Dath: Cordula killt Dich! Oder Wir sind doch nicht Nemesis von jedem Pfeifenheini   Denari: Gyroscopic Horizons   Morris Lapidus. Der Architekt des Amerikanischen Traums   Ellin: Architecture of Fear   Guilbaut: Wie New York die Idee der modernen Kunst gestohlen hat   Hebdige: Subculture. The Meaning of Style   Judin: blank. Architecture, Apartheid And After   Knight: Skinhead   Lee: Object to be destroyed. The Work of Gordon Matta-Clark   Bruce Mau: Life Style   Bauwelt   MVRDV: Costa Iberica. Upbeat to the Leisure City   Baustop.Randstad.- Aggressives, nicht-akkumulatives, städtisches Handeln auf knapp 300 Seiten   Bravo   Oh Snap. The Rap Photography of Ricky Powell   Lipietz: Die grosse Transformation des 21. Jahrtausends. Ein Entwurf der politischen Ökologie   Stevenson: Vacant. A Diary of the Punk Years 1976-79   von Stuckrad-Barre: Livealbum   Clark: The Absolute Bourgeois. Artists and Politics in France 1848-1851   Crimp: Über die Ruinen des Museums. Das Museum, die Fotografie und die Postmoderne   Zingmagazine   Index   Wolkenkratzer Art Journal   Artforum International   Koolhaas, Boeri, Kwinter: Mutations. Arc en Rêve

Freitag 23. bis
Sonntag 25. 11
12.00 bis 22.00 Uhr

Öffnungszeiten
Mo - Fr 13 - 20 Uhr
Sa 12 - 16 Uhr

Musik: Mark Spitz Classics   Coopérateur
T-Ina Darling (Neid)   Rashad   Verena
Heike und Henni   Imran Ayata, Raul Zelik
tazkultur   Wolfgang Renner (Twen FM)
Emotional Quality (Blühendes Barock)
Till   Jochen Becker und Stephan Geene
Dirty Axel   Whirl   Jessif.dat (Jusko Trust)
Dirq   Mo, El Puma (EMD)   Anna Novak
Jörg Hiller   Almut, Fehmi   Thilo (NEU)
Dottore Anore a.k.a forestopper (Tête-à-Tête)
LORD FRIED RICH

etabliert
seit 1999

PRO qm

thematische buchhandlung zu:
Stadt, Politik, Pop, Ökonomie,
Architektur, Design, Kunst & Theorie

alte schönhauser strasse 48
10119 berlin
tel 247 28520 / fax 247 28521
info@pro-qm.de
www.pro-qm.de

Alte Schönhauser Straße 48
D 10119 Berlin

Tel. +49 (30) 247 28520
Fax +49 (30) 247 28521

Mo-Fr. 12-20 Uhr
Sa. 11-16 Uhr

info@pro-qm.de
pro-qm.de

thematische Buchhandlung zu
Stadt, Politik, Pop, Ökonomie,
Architektur, Design, Kunst & Theorie

GRAFIK > INTERFACES SYMPOSIUM UEBER SCHRIFT UND SPRACHE
INFO@AUGENBLUTEN.DE

PRO qm

thematische Buchhandlung zu
Stadt, Politik, Pop, Ökonomie
Architektur, Design, Kunst & Theorie

Alte Schönhauser Str. 48
D-10119 Berlin
geöffnet:
Mo-Fr 12-20 Uhr, Sa 11-16 Uhr

Tel.+49.30.247 28520
Fax +49.30.247 28521
info@pro-qm.de

ab 23. Juli:
Texte, Bilder & Medien
www.pro-qm.de: elektronisches Lesen
Espresso
Veranstaltungen

ab 22. Oktober:
Ausstellungen
www.pro-qm.de: elektronisches Kaufen

PRO qm

ERÖFFNUNG
AM 23.7.1999 19:00

thematische Buchhandlung zu
Stadt, Politik, Pop, Ökonomie,
Architektur, Design, Kunst & Theorie

Alte Schönhauser Straße 48
10119 Berlin
Tel 247 28520 / Fax 247 28521
info@pro-qm.de > www.pro-qm.de

Monatsthema:

Juli: Erlebnis ©
Bücher zur Stadt als Ausstellung mit Paradebaustellen und
Investitionslücken (anläßlich "Berlin - Offene Stadt")

Plus: Geschichtsschreibungen
Überblickssysteme von Anarchie bis Zyklopenmauerwerk

Aug.:   Grundeigentum - Konflikte & Spekulationen,
Zaunkönige & Bundesadler, Familienglück & Bürgerbewußtsein

Sept.:   Partizipation - Beteiligungswünsche und Mitmach-
Programme in Kunst, Architektur und Stadtplanung

Bauhaus in Istanbul, Hochhäuser, Sentimentalität,
Buckminster Fuller, Gender Studio, Form und Neuheiten

SWEDEN GRAPHICS

LOCATION: Stockholm, Sweden

PROFILE: "Sweden Graphics consists of Nille Svensson b.1970 and Magnus Åström b.1969. We founded our company called Sweden Graphics in Stockholm in 1997 after studying together at Konstfack University College of Art, Crafts and Design."

MISSION: "There is no real philosophy behind Sweden Graphics but I think the motto, 'not to make interesting graphic design, but to make graphic design interesting' is a good example of what I would like it to be. I think we are good at getting involved and getting to the point without making too many design-nerdy detours. And I also think we are good at knowing our strengths, which is essential for a good end result. It is important to find your own solutions, not for reasons of integrity but because you will be able to execute them much better than anyone else. I also think that we are good at recognising our solutions as being solutions. I don't know what keeps us going; it's a combination of a need to make a living, a need to feel competent and a need to keep control of what you do with your talent."

CLIENTS: "Mostly advertising agencies, music industry, film production companies, and the usual buyers of graphic design services: H&M, Traktor, Big Magazine, Volkswagen, Smith and Jones Films, onedotzero, Bis Publishing and Ikea."

SMITH AND JONES

CLIENT: Smith and Jones Films, UK and USA

BRIEF: "Create a website to showcase the company's film productions — a sort of online showreel. In general they wanted a warm and unpretentious feeling."

CONCEPT: "We wanted to create a concept that would feel dynamic and interactive. The company can add and remove films as they like and visitors can bake cakes, move everything around and leave messages. All this creates the feeling that the site is alive and in a constant state of change."

SOLUTION: "We wanted to present the films as objects on some sort of canvas, but we wanted them to be among other objects to make them less pretentious. Then we had the idea of the ingredients and baking function. We spent a lot of time creating the logic functions that govern the baking. It is actually quite intricate with different combinations of ingredients leading to different baked results. First we did the website and then we did the corporate profile. The website is crucial, the other elements are more like spin-offs of the website concept."

LESSON: "The most important thing was to keep in mind that returning visitors would get tired of the concept sooner or later, however great our design, and when that happened, it was important that the design didn't slow down or hinder visitors getting to the films. Whenever I see a 'skip intro' button on a site I feel embarrassed on the designers' behalf. Why create something that you already know people are going to skip? If you are aware enough to realise that, then why not skip it straight away in the design stage and save us the trouble?"

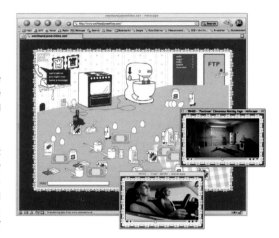

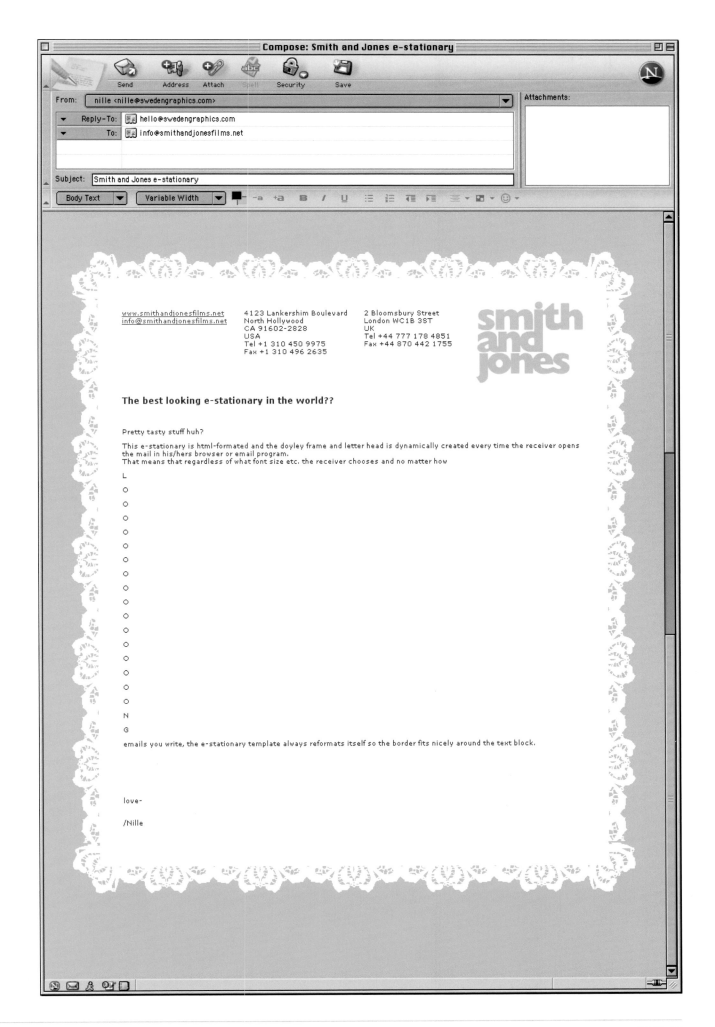

Compose: Smith and Jones e-stationary

Send   Address   Attach   Spell   Security   Save

From: nille <nille@swedengraphics.com>

Reply-To: hello@swedengraphics.com

To: info@smithandjonesfilms.net

Subject: Smith and Jones e-stationary

Attachments:

Body Text   Variable Width

www.smithandjonesfilms.net
info@smithandjonesfilms.net

4123 Lankershim Boulevard
North Hollywood
CA 91602-2828
USA
Tel +1 310 450 9975
Fax +1 310 496 2635

2 Bloomsbury Street
London WC1B 3ST
UK
Tel +44 777 178 4851
Fax +44 870 442 1755

smith and jones

The best looking e-stationary in the world??

Pretty tasty stuff huh?

This e-stationary is html-formated and the doyley frame and letter head is dynamically created every time the receiver opens the mail in his/hers browser or email program.
That means that regardless of what font size etc. the receiver chooses and no matter how

L
O
O
O
O
O
O
O
O
O
O
O
O
O
O
O
O
O
O
N
G

emails you write, the e-stationary template always reformats itself so the border fits nicely around the text block.

love-

/Nille

MARTIN WOODTLI

LOCATION: Zurich, Switzerland

PROFILE: For Woodtli, the beginning of his graphics studies at the School of Design in Berne were a revelation. "The foundation course was incredibly interesting, a completely different world with totally different challenges. It was the first year in my academic life where I had the feeling that I was in the right place and that my own interests were of primary importance, not secondary, as they had been at school." After college, Woodtli spent some time as an intern with Stefan Sagmeister in New York. He then returned to Switzerland in 1999 where he founded his own office.

MISSION: "I find enthusiasm for work to be very important. But I don't think I would do anything else with any less enthusiasm. It doesn't really have anything to do with graphics. I just happened to decide at some point to do graphics and to do it in a way that I want to and not how I am expected to do it. I almost always work alone and am lucky enough to know people who can contribute a bit of hard criticism or discussion. There have been projects that required putting teams together but these situations were one-offs. There is no particular method to my work, like a recipe; in fact that is something I try to avoid. When someone begins to repeat himself, then I get bored – and I don't think I'm the only one."

CLIENTS: Woodtli is particularly active in working with artists while still firmly remaining a designer. "I don't have a particular 'main' client in the usual sense. The Stadtgalerie Bern with its environment of young contemporary art is certainly one of my most long-term clients. Many other projects have arisen from this working environment. Most of them with modest budgets, but for all that, fascinating subjects and people behind them."

SAUERER GROUP

CLIENT: Sauerer Group, Switzerland

BRIEF: The client was a Swiss textile manufacturer. They wanted a series of images for their annual business report. They were particularly keen on Woodtli's visual language and gave him carte-blanche to do the job.

CONCEPT: "To develop a series that was different from the usual illustration commission. Pictures that could stand up for themselves and didn't simply illustrate the text."

SOLUTION: "The result was a business report in print publication format, illustrated with pictures that were not tied to the text."

LESSON: "I got to know about the company itself and how to develop an independent picture series."

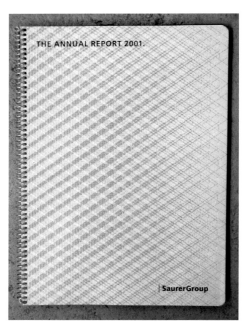

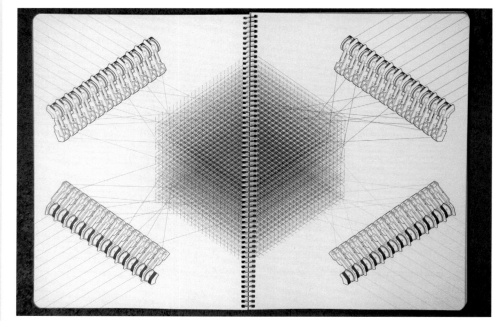

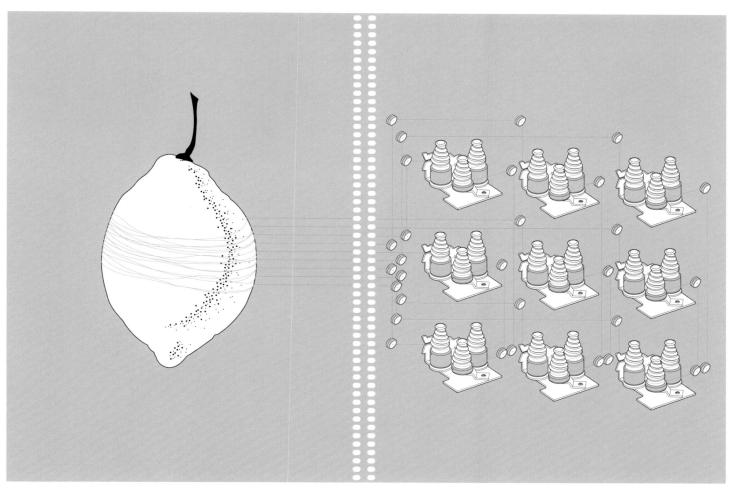

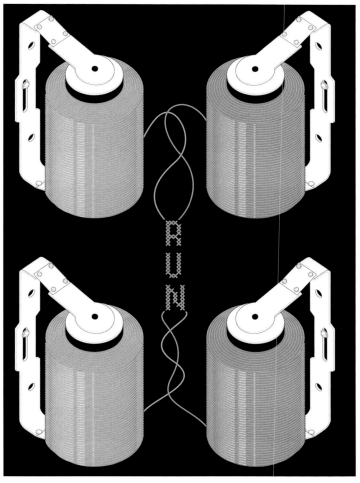

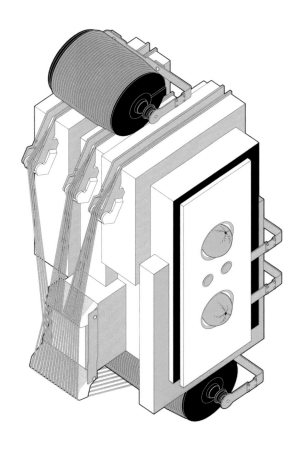

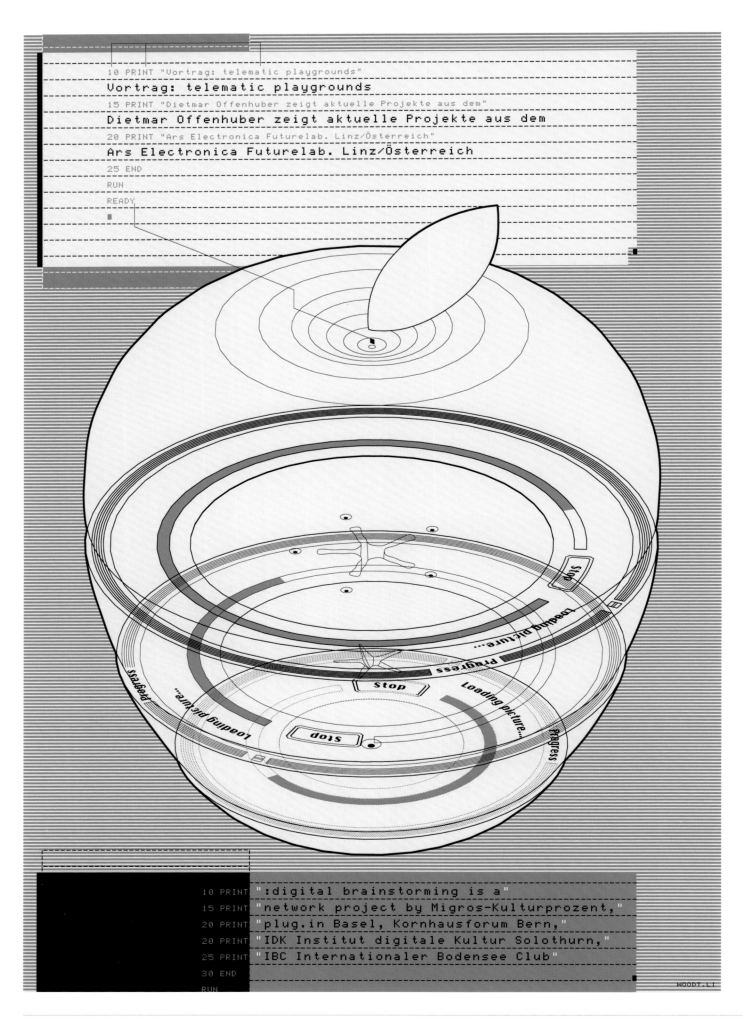

```
10 PRINT "Vortrag: telematic playgrounds"
```
Vortrag: telematic playgrounds
```
15 PRINT "Dietmar Offenhuber zeigt aktuelle Projekte aus dem"
```
Dietmar Offenhuber zeigt aktuelle Projekte aus dem
```
20 PRINT "Ars Electronica Futurelab. Linz/Österreich"
```
Ars Electronica Futurelab. Linz/Österreich
```
25 END
RUN
READY
```

```
10 PRINT ":digital brainstorming is a"
15 PRINT "network project by Migros-Kulturprozent,"
20 PRINT "plug.in Basel, Kornhausforum Bern,"
20 PRINT "IDK Institut digitale Kultur Solothurn,"
25 PRINT "IBC Internationaler Bodensee Club"
30 END
RUN
```

WOODT.LI

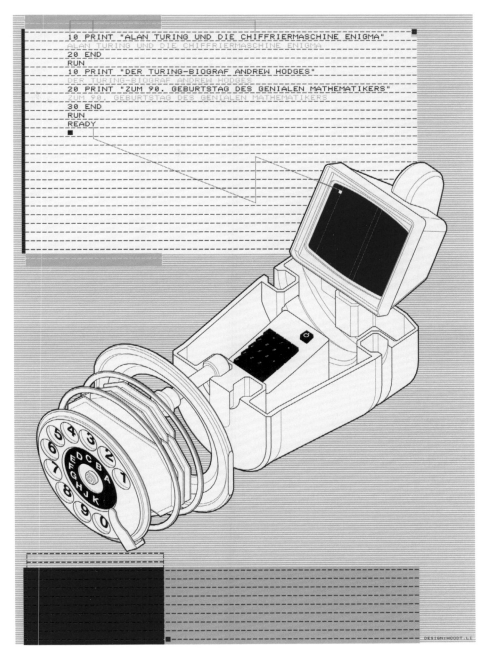

MIGROS KULTURPROZENT

CLIENT: Migros Kulturprozent, Switzerland

BRIEF: Advertising for a lecture series on research and computer culture, with a limited budget

CONCEPT: "To represent the themes using associative constructions."

SOLUTION: "Associative images were created for invitation cards, a website and a CD."

LESSON: "I learned about computer culture and web art."

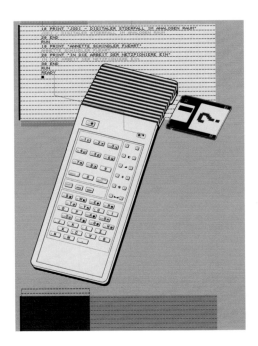

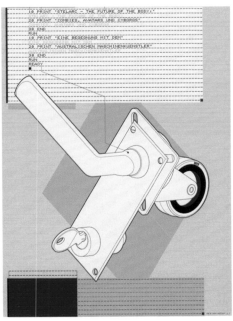

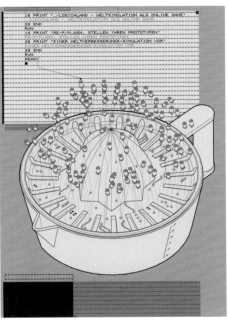

SOLAR
INITIATIVE

LOCATION: Amsterdam, The Netherlands

PROFILE: Solar Initiative, founded and creatively directed by Miguel Gori, Marieke Müskens van Bemmel and Jeannette Zuurbier, is a ten-member team that combines graphic design, website design, interior design, multi-media and photography in one firm.

MISSION: The drive behind Solar Initiative is a quest for the essence of what needs to be communicated. This search is what Solar is built upon, "creating a platform where different creative disciplines can be combined and thus contributing to a continuously evolving creative source". This results in "a clear 'Solar style' of strong conceptual work, with a wide variety of visual interpretations".

CLIENTS: SeARCH Architects, CBK Dordrecht, Modo van Gelder, Delta Lloyd, Delta Lloyd Group, Proof Communications, Sandwich, Orla Kiely London, Rags Industry and Eager Beaver, Roots and Routes, Kèk Media, Lounge, Sic, BNO Spellbound, I-nova, MAG, Diesel, Numico, No Excess, Sodium and Umbrella Architects.

SOLAR CI

CLIENT: Solar Initiative, Amsterdam, The Netherlands

BRIEF: Self-generated initiative to come up with a corporate identity for their own company. "It is important that the choices that are made in Solar Initiative's creative work – the principles of autonomy, experimentation, individuality, essence and a strong starting concept – are expressed in its own house style and promotional materials."

CONCEPT: "The design is based on the reproduction and repetition of 'fake' statistical and scientific data used as illustrations to represent the 'dynamic vision and output' of Solar Initiative. A logo is intentionally not included in this house style; the typography used for the company name is austere and therefore subordinate to the overall style."

SOLUTION: "To emphasise the basic assumption of the concept we chose to use only one print colour – red. The illustrations play a crucial role. Each 'diagram' is different, to underline individuality, experimentation and autonomy." The resulting letterheads, business cards, CD-ROM covers, address stickers etc., come in a wide array of variations. "It is most unlikely anyone will ever receive the same combination, each letter or mailing or invoice or whatever we send will be slightly different and therefore personal, but at the same time always very recognisable as Solar."

LESSON: "You do not necessarily need a logo, or many print colours, to create a strong house style. Focusing on the essence of what you need to communicate and on finding the 'perfect' form or image to express that can lead to unexpected and particularly creative results."

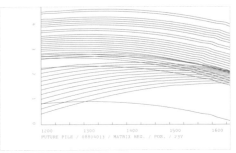

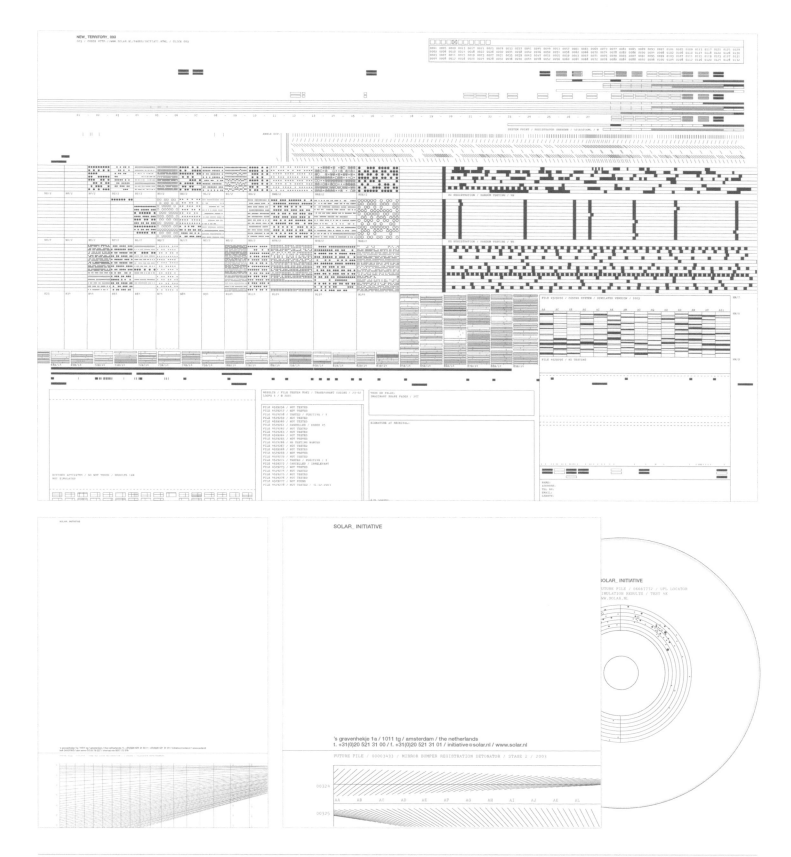

's gravenhekje 1a / 1011 tg / amsterdam / the netherlands
t. +31(0)20 521 31 00 / f. +31(0)20 521 31 01 / initiative@solar.nl / www.solar.nl

MODO VAN GELDER

CLIENT: Modo van Gelder, Amsterdam, The Netherlands

BRIEF: "This wholesale paper company wanted a theme for their annual calendar; something that would make people want to hang it on the wall and actually use it, rather than just chuck it straight in the bin."

CONCEPT: "We discovered that most people who used the calendar worked in environments (like archives, depots and warehouses) where they hardly ever saw any daylight. We thought they could do with a bit of sky, some fun and something other than centre-fold ladies on their calendars."

SOLUTION: "A calendar with lots of fun details to discover every month for its user; a subtle, humour-based graphic, illustrative and textual content. It was so different from what they had before that it stirred things up immensely. People either loved it immediately and praised its sense of understated humour and outspoken graphics, or they hated it, could not relate to it at all and thought it was completely childish. There were two strong camps and therefore it attracted a lot of attention. The client loved the project very much, but later admitted they would have preferred less commotion."

LESSON: "Not everyone has the same sense of humour! But the client stood by us, which we thought was cool and supportive of them."

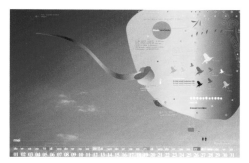

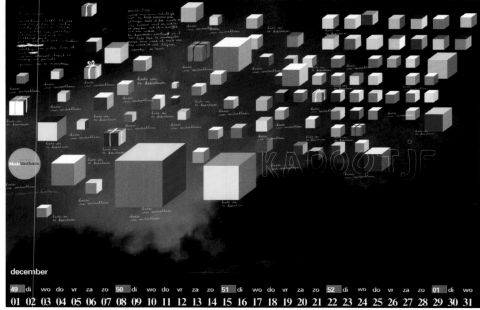

NUDESIGN+
STEFAN YANKU

LOCATION: Adliswil, Switzerland

PROFILE: The recently founded nudesign is a partnership between Stefan Yanku and Achilles Greminger. It focuses on illustration and graphic design, specialising in bilateral/bilingual projects between Japan and Switzerland. Yanku studied basic design and then fashion for two years at the Hochschule für Gestaltung und Kunst in Zurich. He then completed his education via an apprenticeship in a design office and spent four years at MCC Maurer Creative Concepts AG in Zurich. He went to Japan for a year to learn the language and undertake an internship at a Japanese communications agency before returning to Switzerland to take up his partnership with Greminger.

MISSION: Stefan Yanku: "My work is too inspired by other people to be individual, it is more a collage of my environment, things I like mixed together. Of course you might see a particular style in there but I think our environment has a bigger influence on us than we realise. Design has a dialogue with the environment. Design is something that communicates naturally. We have to see it in context, not focus on individuals. That is the way I see design, art and my work."

CLIENTS: The Swiss Japanese Chamber of Commerce, Phile, Roellin Books, Alex Macartney, Umwelteinsatz Schweiz, Matter and Partner AG, Balanx.

USAGI AIR

CLIENT: A self-initiated project devising a corporate identity for a fictional airline company created by Stefan Yanku.

BRIEF: "I had an unclear vision of a 'fashionable' airline that attracts the eye of travellers when the plane is rolling along the runway. I just started and it grew as I worked on it".

CONCEPT: "Tyler Brûlé's redesign of Swissair as 'Swiss' was a kind of blitzkrieg in CD history. A solid concept was created in a very short time for a very complex project. This set me off on the topic of airline design. After the research, I was confronted with the following issues; how to create a difference; how to appeal to customers; how to transmit a sense of security, trust and seriousness in contrast to that of leisure and lifestyle and service and customer care. I built the Usagi Air concept upon my ideal vision of an airline. I looked for a design that incorporated the myth of flying, its pioneer spirit and reflected lifestyle and exclusivity."

SOLUTION: "As impact and atmosphere had priority on this project, I did not begin with a logo or graphic as I usually do, but concentrated on colours and basic shapes. Later I focused on the airplane and uniform design since they are perhaps the most significant carriers of an airline's image. It was very interesting to work 'backwards' and it also eased the process through dealing with many different media, where the concept had to be applicable. Often, the object strongly influenced the graphic; for example the tailplane translated into a belt buckle, which was later a graphic element in the stationery. All the different elements come together best in the uniform; plane shapes, graphics and atmospheric elements inspired by the 1950s."

LESSON: "The interdisciplinary factor of the project forced me to reconsider my usual workflow. I had to learn to begin with simple things and find a general description instead of rushing for a concrete and detailed design."

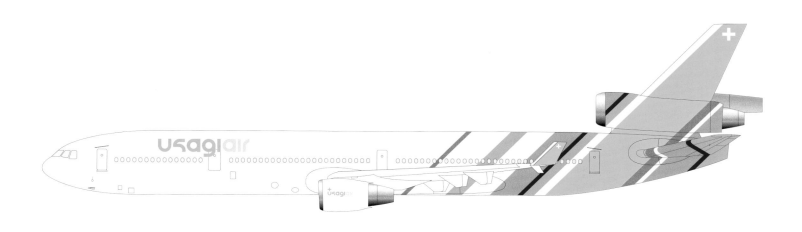

2 Education

Go Buy the Book

What relevance do the traditional career routes of a college education, an internship, and the cultivation of a classy Curriculum Vitae have to contemporary designers? Surely there's more to be learned online and on the streets than in the fusty halls of academia or a large agency loft space? As much as work practices and disciplines may have changed, it seems that our views on education are often not far off those that our grandparents might have had.

Do you have to go to college to be a good designer? Isn't it better to go your own way and learn by experience?

DAG HENNING BRANDSAETER: "On the one hand I think it's great when one takes the initiative to learn by experience and is motivated by passion, but on the other hand I believe college is a great place to experiment, play, and evolve, as well as to build bridges, and create networks of like-minded creatives. I believe it's very important to maintain one's artistic side; to keep playing, keep experimenting. There are also certain aspects of the profession, such as typography, which I believe require theoretical training, either by studying with mentors or from books."

KASIA KORCZAK: "College provides the intellectual framework and accountability that is too often lacking in design. It enables you to understand why you are doing what you are doing instead of simply relying on intuition alone."

FULGURO: "College is a good way to meet interesting people, teachers as well as students, and to be in contact with different disciplines (graphics, industrial design, film, fine art etc.). It is important to be curious. It is also a way of building a personal network and getting in touch with people from other places."

ANDY MUELLER: "You do not HAVE to go to college to be a good designer. I went to college but not to an art school and I have yet to take a design class. I'm not necessarily proud of this, it's just the way it is. I think it's quite possible to go your own way and learn by looking a things, reading books, experimenting with projects, and by learning as you go."

JORG ANDRE DIETER: "I can only speak from my own experience in Berlin, but I found it a shame that the best people did not teach at my college were . I also think that to study five years is far too long. I didn't like being in a position (at school or at college) where other people were making the decisions for me."

JONATHAN BARNBROOK: "I don't ever care about qualifications. I look at the person more than anything else. The portfolio is probably about half of it but the person is extremely important. Whether they are a passionate or they are a nice person, you know. It's no good being a good designer if you are a git."

KENZO MINAMI: "The worst thing is going to school and not knowing where you stand culturally and philosophically as well as not having your own aesthetic, views and beliefs. It's like going online and starting to surf the Web without knowing what you are looking for. I don't think anyone should go to art school before they know where they stand."

Do you have to study design to be a good designer or are apprenticeships still a valid form of education?

DAG HENNING BRANDSAETER: "If you have strong ambitions, and passion for what you do, then theoretical training is not required. I believe you get enough training through internships etc. to evolve and become just as good as anyone with a degree."

FULGURO: "Design is an open and broad discipline. In college you learn how to look at things in various ways, not how to make them. And after all, what is a good designer anyway?"

KENZO MINAMI: "I never took a class in Fine Art or graphic design in my life. I taught myself just because I was (and still am) simply curious. If you are curious enough, you can learn theory and skill anywhere. But the whole point of paying to go to school is that you get an amazing amount of access to facilities, information and the experience of teachers (if that helps you in any way at all) and if you use it wisely, it can be a huge advantage."

If college, then does "which college" matter? Does having studied at Central Saint Martins, the RCA or écal, for example, give you a calling card to success?

DAG HENNING BRANDSAETER: "[It matters] in the same way that a hip address does, but if the portfolio doesn't meet requirements, then the school makes no difference at all."

FULGURO: "Yes, it does matter. Was écal a good college? It depends on the year you were there. Our year had a great time; there were very few in our class (8 diploma students), so we could have long hours of discussion with our teachers Ronan Bouroullec and Radi Designers. No, it is not a calling card to success, but it is a good way to meet interesting people and to stimulate your curiosity."

ANDY MUELLER: "I have no idea, it hasn't mattered all my life. No one ever asks me what school I went to. All people want to see is my work."

JONATHAN BARNBROOK: "Unfortunately I think it does make a difference. I think what those [first] two colleges give you is confidence more than anything else. Design and advertising have a lot to do with confidence. When you walk into an interview with a client or to get a job, if you have a relaxed attitude, which comes from an education where people make you believe in yourself, then it does make a difference. But I try and be fair to all people – none of the people working in my studio went to the Royal College or St. Martins – except me."

How valid are internships? What are applicants looking for? A well-organised office where they can learn practical tips about client acquisition and running jobs, or do they prefer to choose chaotic creatives as inspirational mentors?

DAG HENNING BRANDSAETER: "I can imagine that the first thing they are looking for is a well-known studio, which will look good on their C.V. Then they want to play and make nice things, which (due to the ever-present tight deadlines and budgets) will make them do some training in actual practice; dealing with project managers and account executives breathing down their necks."

JONATHAN BARNBROOK: "I think that when people come here it is not that different from college, which is probably the opposite of what many people want. There isn't as much time as there is at college but there is time to have some good ideas and it isn't structured in such a business-like way. Being in a studio is one of the best things a student can do."

Who looks at C.V.s these days, are they still relevant or have they been superceded by the homepage?

DAG HENNING BRANDSAETER: "I think a C.V. is still important. It is proof of how ambitious you are, and what you've accomplished over the years."

FULGURO: "A C.V. is the old school, systematic way valid for huge companies; the other and more personal route would be an interview, a book or a homepage. In the field of Design a C.V. is very reductive."

KENZO MINAMI: "I have luckily never encountered a situation in which I had to show my C.V. and I don't even have a website. I seem to get projects from clients who have seen my latest work and sometimes that's all they really have seen. This does not necessarily make the situation easy, since it makes you do every single project as if it is to replace your entire C.V. So I guess what would be better than C.V.s and homepages would be to approach every project as if it were the best project you've ever done or the project you will always be known for."

If you did go to college, how was the jump from being in the theory-laden, experimental life in the education cocoon to the shock of starting out in an agency or going freelance for the first time?

DAG HENNING BRANDSAETER: "I actually did two internships, one while I was at college, and one after graduation. The contrast between them was huge. I think what shocked me the most the first time, was the hierarchy in the office, the strict deadlines and annoying project managers who didn't let me play around enough. But when I better understood how things really work, everything got a bit clearer. I figured out that it's all about doing the best you can so that the work you produce satisfies your as well as the client's needs."

FULGURO: "It was such a big jump that we don't know if we have landed yet. On the other hand it was quite transitional as our first job was an animation for Ronan and Erwan Bouroullec, which was really personal and non-commercial. Still, it's good to keep going on the experimental track. It is our 'material' for other jobs. We need it although we have less and less time for it."

JONATHAN BARNBROOK: "In a practical sense, it was very difficult because I didn't have the time, facilities or people to discuss projects with. But in a determination sense, it wasn't any different. One of the big things that happens is that people's ideas get watered down after leaving college. It is very difficult to sustain them if you have practicalities like earning money to deal with. Also you absolutely become your own judge after leaving college and if you are not completely applied to what you want to do, then it can all get lost in just trying to finish work and trying to do something 'nice'. You are free to do as you please and that can be quite dangerous."

What happens when all that theory you learned meets the harsh world of practice?

DAG HENNING BRANDSAETER: "After a while it all falls into place. But at the beginning it was quite frustrating because making compromises can be quite hard, especially when working with tight budgets and deadlines on exciting projects."

FULGURO: "Nothing. Theory and practice are often too far away from each other to interact anyway."

FULGURO

LOCATION: Lausanne, Switzerland

PROFILE: After graduating in Industrial Design from the École Cantonale d'Art de Lausanne (écal) in 2001, Cédric Decroux, Axel Jaccard and Yves Fidalgo launched straight into working together on a collection of prestige projects. First up was the Pavilion Territoire Imaginaire in Bienne for the Expo.02 for which they called themselves "Waterproof". This was closely followed by an installation film project called Motion Notebook for French superstar designers Ronan and Erwan Bouroullec in the London Design Museum. Now operating under the name "Fulguro", the trio continue to go from strength to strength and already have a solo exhibition in Lausanne and an Ikea chair in their portfolio.

CONTEXT: Fulguro's output covers a broad bandwidth; they think nothing of tackling bespoke furniture design one moment, then packaging, product design, graphics, CI, animation, or plain old graphics the next. In their own words, they "mix many fields and disturb disciplines".

CLIENTS: Atelier OÏ (visual identity and website), Iril (new concept for collection catalogues and website), JJZ Architekten (reHOUSE project collaboration), Ikea (Bölja long chair design), It Design (furniture catalogue).

LES URBAINES

CLIENT: Les Urbaines Festival, Lausanne, Switzerland

BRIEF: To create a new visual identity, logo, poster, programme etc. for the festival. There were nine different locations to signpost. The signposts had to give the festival a tangible presence in the city. The clients had been using the same identity for the past six years and they wanted something fresh, new and poetic.

CONCEPT: "We created an imaginary character especially for the event – a building painter. He went through the city getting the various locations ready for the festival. It gave us inspiration for the visuals as well as for the objects and interventions at the various sites. The character left a trail behind him of marks and tools, like clues to his presence; spreading the festival's identity almost imperceptibly."

SOLUTION: A huge-scale poster showing the painter getting the poster ready. A programme in booklet / fanzine format showing the different places being prepared for the festival and introducing the events. Limited-edition rolls of sticky tape used for all the installations and signs in the city. An uncut version of the printed programme left in large sheets and used for protecting or wrapping the locations like a painter would do before painting. A new font called Adhesive.

RESULT: Every component was linked to the main character. The sticky tape was particularly welcome and helped spread the festival's identity throughout the city.

LESSON: "Low budget is the best you can get! Everything was ready on time."

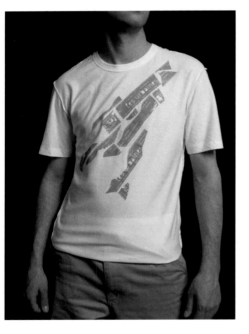

SOCKS AND STOCKINGS

CLIENT: IRIL Services, Renens, Switzerland

BRIEF: To develop wholesale catalogues for the new collections of a Swiss hosiery manufacturer in a limited edition of 50. The difficulty was that there was a large range of products to represent, that the series was small and that there were many last-minute changes to the collections.

CONCEPT: "To represent the different styles using hand-drawn images inspired by characters and places found in magazines and mixing them to create a new atmosphere. The images of the tights and socks were integrated into the drawings in such a way as to emphasise the products and not the drawings themselves".

SOLUTION: The catalogue ended up being a folder with a metal ring in the middle. The collection was a pack of sheets to stick in the folder every new season. Every product was represented on a separate sheet to facilitate easy addition or removal of products, last-minute changes and the addition of special sheets such as colour samples.

RESULT: "A pure and simple visual identity, quick to make and with low-budget materials. The client asked us for a second catalogue after the first winter collection."

LESSON: "Laser prints and photocopies can give good results."

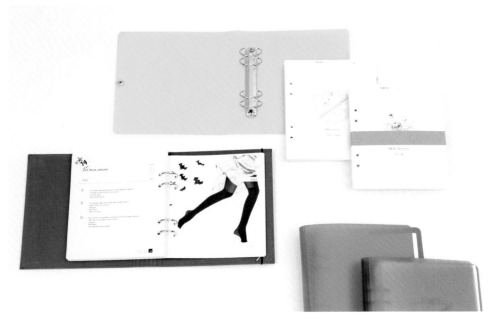

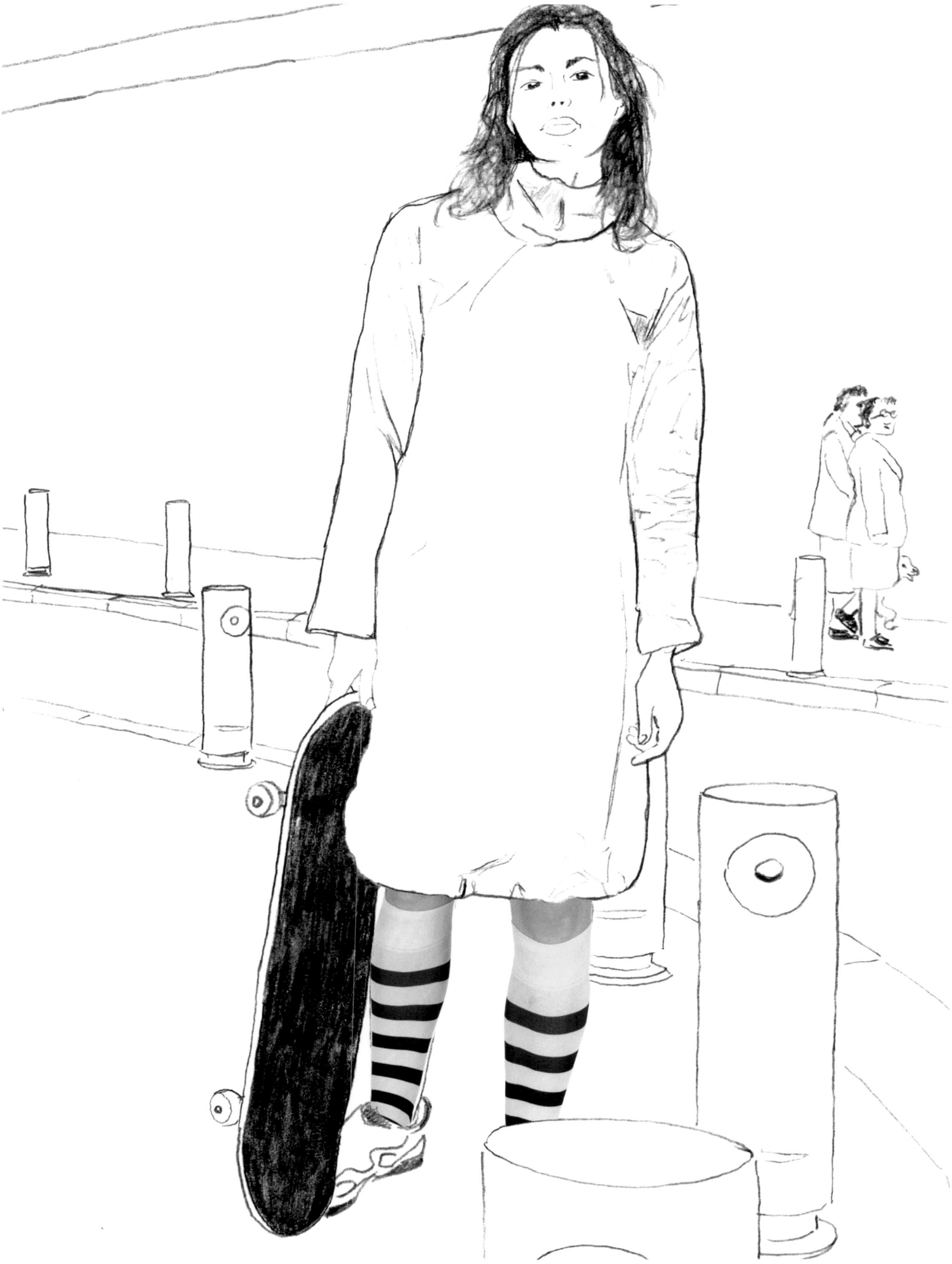

DIPESH PANDYA

LOCATION: Paris, France

PROFILE: Of Indian parentage but born in Dar-es-Salaam, Tanzania, Pandya grew up in Leicester in England and studied at Central Saint Martins in London. After graduating, he moved to Paris in 1993 where he worked for Citizen K and Vogue Hommes International as Assistant Art Director. He then took a position as Art Director for the launch of Jalouse USA before deciding to take a break from the ego-driven world of fashion magazines and concentrate more on the music industry.

MISSION: "My style is freestyle. I'm a loner and have tried working with a team but it is too complicated and gets boring after a while. It's very difficult to find people you can really work with. I like to think I have a 'no compromise' policy but the fact is that I am flexible to a certain degree within my original idea but if it gets too compromised then it's time to decide whether I pull out or continue. On many recent projects I have had a 'soft' no-compromise method that has worked well for both my clients and myself."

CLIENTS: Palais de Tokyo, France; Groupe Hachette Filipacchi Photos, France; Common & Sense, Japan; United Arrows, Japan; Sound of Barclay, Universal Music, France; Studio K7!, Germany; Big Dada, Ninja Tune, England; Vorston and Limantell, BMG, France; Virgin, France; Inca Music, France; Le Colette No.3 Juillet 2003, France; Ashes, France; Pépé, France; Rossignol and Le Coq Sportif by Jean-Charles de Castelbajac, France.

PLAYLIST

CLIENT: Palais de Tokyo, Site de Creation Contemporaine, Paris, France

BRIEF: "The exhibition was curated by one of the Directors of the Palais de Tokyo, Nicolas Bourriaud. His idea was to feature artists who work with cultural products rather than raw materials. Playlist is not a show illustrating a theme but a variation on a working principle (or rather a mental structure) that we might call cultural navigation, i.e. the artist is a research engine manoeuvring among signs."

CONCEPT: "The idea was to translate the Playlist concept into a book / magazine format serving as a catalogue for the exhibition. My idea was to give an effect of layers of information that the reader is forced to sort through. My original idea was to print the whole catalogue on transparent plastic sheets – way too expensive!"

SOLUTION: "One of the first ideas consisted of using sections, each with various page sizes; again dealing with the notion of layering. The final translucent, iridescent, plastic cover was the best solution for me in terms of translating this idea within the constraints of the budget. The use of over 40 different typefaces also enhanced this feeling."

LESSON: "It had been a couple of years since I had stopped art directing magazines so getting back into a magazine / catalogue format with over 200 pages was very difficult at first."

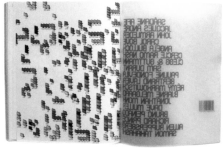

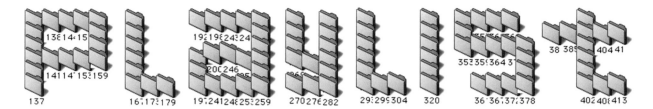

PALAIS DE TOKYO
site de création contemporaine
www.palaisdetokyo.com

12 FEV – 25 AVR 2004

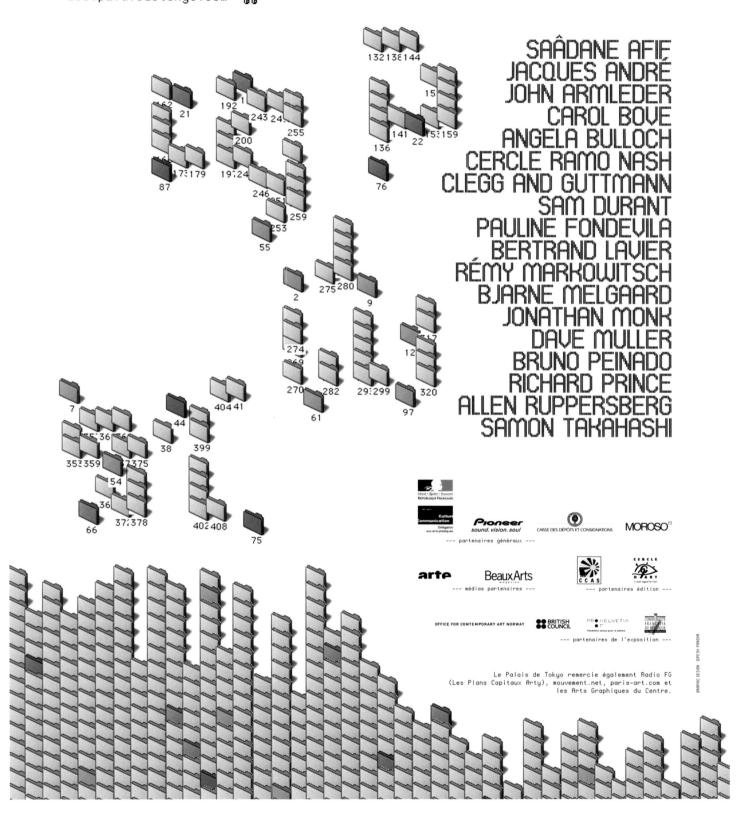

SAÂDANE AFIF
JACQUES ANDRÉ
JOHN ARMLEDER
CAROL BOVE
ANGELA BULLOCH
CERCLE RAMO NASH
CLEGG AND GUTTMANN
SAM DURANT
PAULINE FONDEVILA
BERTRAND LAVIER
RÉMY MARKOWITSCH
BJARNE MELGAARD
JONATHAN MONK
DAVE MULLER
BRUNO PEINADO
RICHARD PRINCE
ALLEN RUPPERSBERG
SAMON TAKAHASHI

RÉPUBLIQUE FRANÇAISE

Culture Communication
Délégation aux arts plastiques

Pioneer
sound. vision. soul.

CAISSE DES DÉPÔTS ET CONSIGNATIONS

MOROSO

--- partenaires généraux ---

arte

BeauxArts magazine

CCAS

CERCLE D'ART
L'autre regard sur l'art

--- médias partenaires ---   --- partenaires édition ---

OFFICE FOR CONTEMPORARY ART NORWAY

BRITISH COUNCIL

PRO HELVETIA
Fondation suisse pour la culture

COMMUNAUTÉ FRANÇAISE DE BELGIQUE

--- partenaires de l'exposition ---

Le Palais de Tokyo remercie également Radio FG
(Les Plans Capitaux Arty), mouvement.net, paris-art.com et
les Arts Graphiques du Centre.

GRAPHIC DESIGN: DIPESH PANDYA

SOPHIE TOPORKOFF

LOCATION: Paris, France

PROFILE: Sophie Toporkoff studied at ESAG / Penninghen in Paris, where she graduated in 1999, but she also spent a year at the Hochschule der Künste in Berlin in 1998 and a year at the School of Visual Arts in New York in 2000. After college she skipped the internship phase and went straight into freelancing. Her work covers a range of fields including art direction, graphic design, illustration, painting, writing and music videos.

MISSION: "My 'structure' is to work alone, but I love to collaborate with different people on different projects. For example, for the magazine AGENDA I work with the publisher, the editor and lots of photographers and illustrators. For the Colette magazine, I did the art direction with Dipesh Pandya and the illustration with Fafi, and for the 'LIVE' exhibition catalogue for Palais de Tokyo, I worked with all the crew at the institution and Agnes Dehan for the photographs. So, I work with many different people, but never a regular group."

CLIENTS: Coca-Cola, Colette, Eurostar, Hotel Pershing Hall, OFR, Palais de Tokyo, Universal Music, Van Cleef and Arpels, Versatile, etc.

AGENDA

CLIENT: AGENDA, Paris, France

BRIEF: Graphic design and art direction for a new fashion, music and culture magazine. "This project is very special. It was launched together with Alexandre Thumerelle, editor, and Sophie Berbar-Sollier, editor-in-chief. We are really free to do whatever we want."

CONCEPT: "Our only goal is to say and show as many interesting and beautiful things about Paris as possible – the city where we live and the city that we love."

SOLUTION: "To show modern and beautiful images. To be honest and not tricky. I want to share images and ideas with the readers. I present images by people I really admire such as Camille Vivier, Mark Borthwick, Lobato, Olivier Amsellem and Pierre la Police...and I have created a layout for the kind of magazine that I always wanted to see."

LESSON: "Not hesitating to contact people who's work I really admire and asking them to work with us."

Cover: Lobato

Fashion Story: Lobato

Fashion Story: Lobato

LIVE

CLIENT: Palais de Tokyo, Site de Création Contemporaine, Paris, France

BRIEF: "To design a catalogue for the 'LIVE' exhibition. Jérôme Sans, the curator, wanted a very 'lively' catalogue – a 'bomb' as he liked to say."

CONCEPT: "The idea was to produce a catalogue in which you could 'feel' the music, so I wanted to create graphic surprises. This was the third catalogue that I had designed for the Palais de Tokyo, so the main challenge was to keep on coming up with new ideas and not reproducing what I had already done for 'Hardcore' and 'GNS'. On the other hand, working for Jérôme Sans was quite comfortable since we had already worked together. I knew what he liked and he knew what I was capable of."

SOLUTION: "I created a simple overall layout and changed a lot of details in each section to keep the reader's eye busy. Firstly, each artist's name was hand-written as graffiti, then the idea of having a fluorescent yellow section at the beginning and the end of the catalogue came quite quickly. I really liked the effect of black and white pictures printed on the colour – very 'live'. There were no borders to images to accentuate the 'bold' effect. I didn't want to produce too many design effects with the images. All these images finally came together really well, it looked pretty much like how I had imagined; lots of things to look at in a simple layout and a certain kind of anarchy without being a punk cliché – staying modern."

LESSON: "I collaborated with the crew at the Palais de Tokyo and everyone had their own ideas about this catalogue so it was a very interactive process. I learned to listen to everyone's opinion, learn from them yet still keep hold of my own strong ideas."

MK12

LOCATION: Kansas City, USA

PROFILE: MK12 is a team of nine people who work primarily in motion graphics and broadcast design. They also create their own short films and original content, some print work and experimental design. Most of the team met while studying at the Kansas City Art Institute and continued to work together on short film projects after graduating. After about a year of working at various jobs in the industry they decided to go into business for themselves and officially founded MK12 in 2000.

MISSION: "Our only philosophy is not to have a philosophy. We are constantly changing and adapting ourselves to our environment, our inspirations, etc. So long as we stay happy with the work that we produce and feel that we are challenging ourselves and others, that's what matters most."

CLIENTS: MTV, Adidas, AXN, SciFi Channel, Schematic Records, SubPop Records.

ANATOMY OF RECEPTACLES

CLIENT: Paragraph Gallery, Kansas City, USA

BRIEF: "The gallery asked artists to create a piece pertaining to a theme; the construction of space whether architectural, graphic, urban, social, public, private, personal, virtual, slow or controlled."

CONCEPT: The concept was devised and executed by Maiko Kuzunishi. "My approach to the theme was a metacognitive and metaphysical idea of space, expressed as a container that holds whatever or however we define ourselves as individuals. It was mainly about asking, 'what is true self?' in its pure form."

SOLUTION: "After brainstorming several ideas, I ended up having two banners and 128 boxes, each containing a crumpled screen print. The banners were used to attract attention to the stacked boxes and to give an analogy of the concept. Two faceless figures deprived of identity stand in front of the rich patterns representing mixtures of content. Real boxes were stacked in the space, labelled with a price tag of US$5 and were for sale during the show. Each box contained a crumpled screen print. Physically crumpling the paper devalues the content and, hopefully, draws attention back to the container itself."

LESSON: "The whole process of creation was a big learning process. It was about pushing my own limits and creatively freeing myself from my known formula; the usual way I do things."

ANTOINE + MANUEL

LOCATION: Paris, France

PROFILE: "There are just two of us, as the name implies. We are both French; Antoine is more involved with fashion and Manuel with design. We met at art college just after graduation, we felt in love, and have been living together ever since. After a couple of years work experience, we decided to work together and created our own company: Antoine+Manuel."

MISSION: "We are kind of 'image directors', in that we simultaneously produce drawings (graphic design and illustration), typography, logos, photos, furniture, stage sets, displays, packaging and so on. Antoine is more intuitive and Manuel more conceptual, but sometimes the roles are totally reversed. Even though we are very close to each other, we retain our individual goals. You could say that we like to produce something really involved in its own time, yet with the thought that it can still be interesting twenty years from now. We always keep in mind that the objects we create are aimed at an audience, and we want to provoke emotions. Since we are our first audience, this emotion has to work on us."

CLIENTS: Christian Lacroix and Hedi Slimane for Yves Saint Laurent, Collection Lambert, Musée d'Art Moderne de la ville de Paris, Centre Pompidou, Musée des Arts Décoratifs Paris, Centre Chorégraphique National de Tours (CCNT), National Theatre of Dijon, Comedie de Clermont-Ferrand, Yvon Lambert Gallery, Fiac, Habitat, Lafayette Maison.

COLLECTION LAMBERT

CLIENT: Collection Lambert, Avignon, France

BRIEF: Design a poster series for a new contemporary art museum. "At the beginning, in 2000, they let us have a very free rein. We had worked with these clients in the past, so we were quite familiar with each other. Since it was a totally new museum, we had to invent a corporate image too."

CONCEPT: "The goal was to create an identity which could give the feeling that contemporary art is for everybody, not only for connoisseurs. At first, the idea was to make each poster like a teenager's own drawing of the artwork's of famous artists. Drawing is about appropriation, like eating or touching something. It was the first time that Antoine used his personal drawing in a corporate identity project."

SOLUTION: "It was Manuel's idea and he asked Antoine to do the drawings. The artists loved the drawings of their artworks and the public was really touched. Only the other curators were sceptical; they said that making an artwork from an artwork was breaking a taboo. Now, four years later, this identity is famous among French museums, and recognised by the local public."

LESSON: "With this project we've learnt that sometimes people have taboos that don't break easily, even in the rarified world of contemporary art."

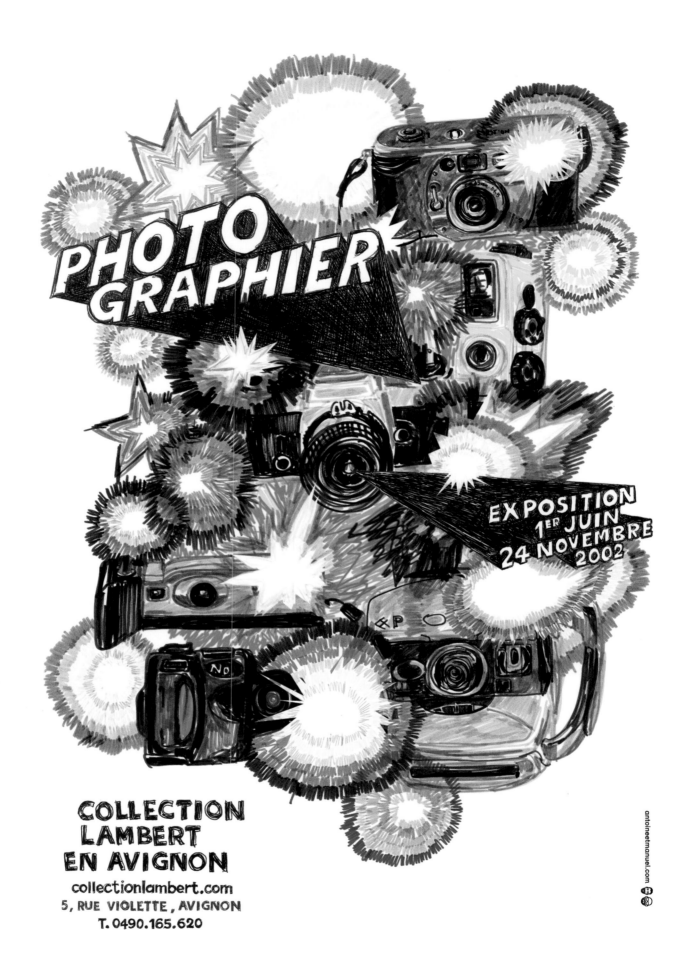

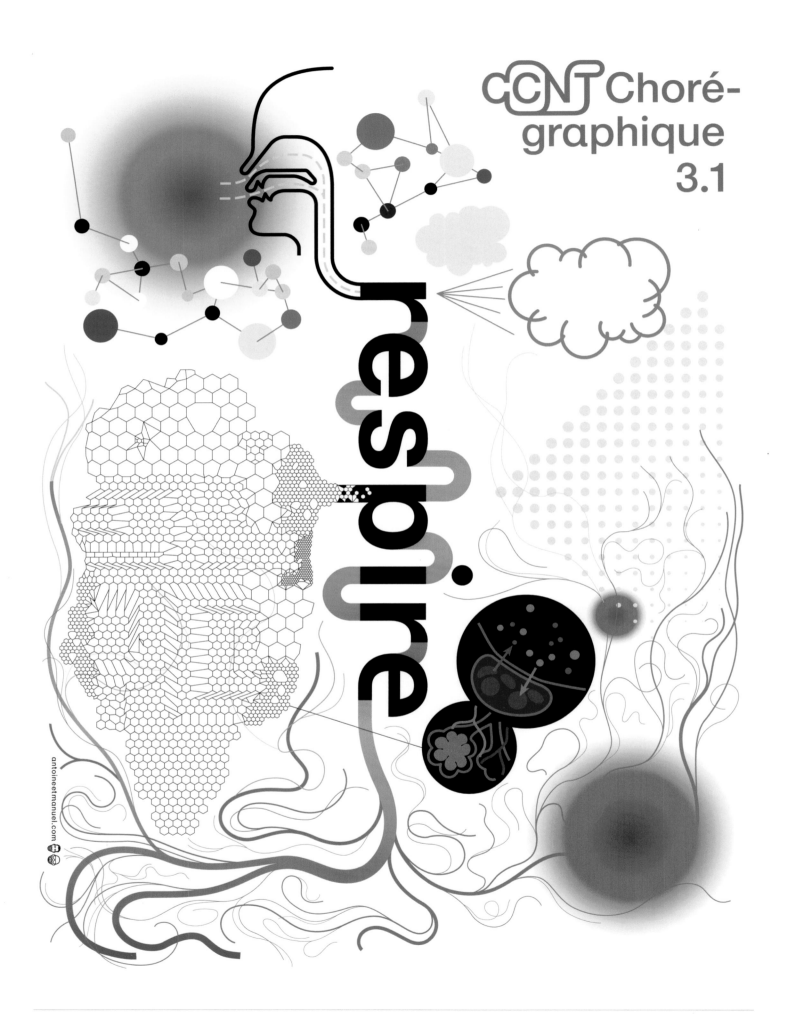

cCNT Choré-
graphique
3.1

respire

antoineetmanuel.com

CHORÉ-GRAPHIQUE

CLIENT: Centre Chorégraphique National de Tours, France

BRIEF: "The client (the choreographer Daniel Larrieu) asked us to come up with a new type of communication for the choreography centre that he has been Director of for the past nine years. Previously, the Choré-graphique had been an annual festival; now it has a dance programme throughout the year."

CONCEPT: "To find a different way of communicating dance without using photographs of dancers. Almost a year before, I had designed a modified version of Helvetica with ornaments. I wanted to take this further and have the illustration coming out of the letters."

SOLUTION: "A programme with seasonal information that is, at the same time, a poster. The public quickly fell in love with the posters. They waited for the each one (three per year, nine in total), and hung them on their walls."

LESSON: "Keep going straight ahead and do not be influenced by bad ideas around you. The communication director was really helpful throughout the project and became a close and beloved friend. We're now working together for another choreographic centre, the CNDC, in Angers, France."

WINDOW DISPLAY

CLIENT: Galeries Lafayette (Lafayette Maison), Paris, France

BRIEF: "At first, the client wanted us to design shop windows inspired by our works for the CCNT and our drawings for Christian Lacroix. He also felt that they should refer to fashion, since Galeries Lafayette call themselves a 'fashion department store'. He allowed us to be really free, and accepted our first project, even though it was quite different from what he had in mind."

CONCEPT: "We wanted to mix illustration and space. The idea came easily because it was an ancient idea and part of our everyday work. We wanted to make something like an illustration that became a whole artificial, magical universe."

SOLUTION: "We made podia to raise the designer furniture up higher. We decided to show only one piece of furniture per window. Then we composed 2D illustrations from stripes, regular dots and flowers (cut out of fluorescent coloured vinyl foil) mixed with 3D geometric flowers (black and fluorescent blue and green lacquered wood). We also added a series of different disco lighting systems so at night, the shop windows looked totally different, with rapidly flashing coloured lights. It was our first major shop window."

LESSON: "It confirmed to us that we enjoy creating spatial projects."

3 Location

Hubs, Ports + Bases

How important is "location" to a designer or illustrator? Which country, which city, uptown or downtown, should you be in a "happening" district or close to the "street"? Or does the fact that we are all data-networked via our computers mean that location is a redundant issue? If that were the case wouldn't most of us be living in countryside idylls or next to our favourite beach? Designers need clients, inspiration, a peer group and a place to work, but sometimes not all of these are to be found on the same continent, let alone in the same city.

Are locations inspiring and do they effect creative output by having an effect on input?
DAG HENNING BRANDSAETER: "To me they absolutely are. One of my biggest inspirations is the environment that surrounds me, from the daily impulses from people you meet, to places you go and visit. I also believe that if you are comfortable and inspired by the atmosphere that you're in, it will show in your work. I need a dynamic environment, with new impulses and input every day in order to keep evolving, If everything stayed static and the same it would end up being a routine job and I would stagnate and be left with no inspiration."

MICHAEL SPOLJARIC, PHANTOM:RESEARCH-FOUNDATION: "Location takes a back seat to the quality of work the company / illustrator does. If you are good and work in one of the major cities then that is like gold dust. If your work is shit but you are in a good location then it can still work to your advantage."

MARCO FIEDLER, VIER5: "I think location isn't that important. Hip locations never really interested us. A location is as important as one likes to make it, even when it is just lying on the sofa with a piece of pizza in your hand. Being close to the street can be important, but by that I mean being close to life – you should be close to life."

Do you need to be near your clients?
FLORIAN PFEFFER, JUNG + PFEFFER: "Yes, more than ever. It was one of the big mistakes of the dot.com society to believe that technology could replace human contact."

STEFAN YANKU: "This is something I ask myself too. On one hand, we can communicate via phone or email, but from time to time personal contact is essential to keep the relationship alive or to discuss projects effectively. When I was in Japan for over a year, the relation-ships and the progress of my Swiss projects suffered tremendously. Emails and phone calls reduce information transfer to a minimum and hardly encourage an inspiring conversation. In terms of sales, I doubt that is possible to win a customer without meeting them at least once – and at some key stages of projects, personal meetings are more effective."

KASIA KORCZAK: "Yes, one needs to be near clients for periodic meetings and to give them a sense of presence. So you can if need be, come face to face with the client. That said, the bulk of my design work takes place in cities other than those of the client, whether in Poland, Italy or France."

DAG HENNING BRANDSAETER: "I feel it is good to have a personal relationship with the client in the sense that there is often much that is left unsaid in email or video conferences. I think it is easier and better to know where you stand with your client and which direction to take by also analysing his or her 'body language'."

Is a hip address as important as the right URL for attracting jobs?
STEFAN YANKU: "London or Oberleimbach, Paris or Wädenschwil? What a question. We are all – including me – too simple-minded and believe in status and reputation. But in the end it's just a matter of coolness and not really necessary. The quality of the work is what attracts the customers. But I think the offices should be in a more or less convenient location."

MARCO FIEDLER, VIER5: "I think particular places exert a particular attraction and fascination and that can naturally have a positive effect on work. On the other hand you should not place too much value on it: you can't judge good work by a postcode."

DAG HENNING BRANDSAETER: "I think location, name, image etc. is important in the sense that it will certainly give you an advantage in telling others which direction you and your studio wish to be heading."

Is it important to be near other like-minded designers and "creatives"?
MICHAEL SPOLJARIC, PHANTOM:RESEARCH-FOUNDATION: "For me yes! I am way out in Oregon and I feel a bit more out of touch than when I was in New York. Perhaps it can be a good thing too, I will have to get back to you on this. Some artists go into isolation and then really kick ass…"

MARCO FIEDLER, VIER5: "No, but it feels good to know that particular people are nearby."

Is it good or bad for business when all the city's creatives are located within the same block?
MARCO FIEDLER, VIER5: "Exchange is good of course, but too much proximity can be damaging. Sometimes an email is enough. I don't think living cheek to cheek is important; neighbours that work in other fields are often much more interesting."
MICHAEL SPOLJARIC, PHANTOM:RESEARCH-FOUNDATION: "I have no idea. Look at the garment district in New York. Most of the fashion design comes from that area and business seems good. Some companies do well in this environment and the quality of work gets better."
KASIA KORCZAK: "There is a certain conformity or homogeneity that results when creatives are all based in one area."
DAG HENNING BRANDSAETER: "Different locations mean different impulses and different ways of working."
FLORIAN PFEFFER, JUNG + PFEFFER: "It is good for business to work in an environment of quality. A city, region or country with a strong creative industry creates clients, jobs and opportunities. It is wrong to believe that it is harder to find your own slot in a city with a lot of competition. It is much harder to work in a place without good examples and therefore with an underdeveloped understanding of design and communication; you would have no references and would always be struggling to explain what you are doing."

Are certain cities better for certain branches e.g. Paris for illustrators or Hamburg for graphic designers?
MICHAEL SPOLJARIC, PHANTOM:RESEARCH-FOUNDATION: "No, I doubt that any one city has a style-on-lock 100% but some do lead in certain branches: London has the record covers and L.A. does the film titles (not that half of them are any good), for example."
STEFAN YANKU: "The ideal place is where I feel comfortable and where my customers are."
DAG HENNING BRANDSAETER: "In terms of networking you may want to go to a city that is known for its talent pool in a particular field that you specialise in or wish to be heading towards. But for more established designers,

or studios, a presence in the 'right' location in terms of acquiring clients and staying up to date etc. sounds to me like a bit of a redundant issue because we already have easy access to these places though data networking."

Do members of a design team need to be in the same building, city or country anymore? What are the advantages or disadvantages of being a company or team spread over several cities, or even continents?
FLORIAN PFEFFER, JUNG + PFEFFER: "For me, it is rather a disadvantage being spread over cities and continents. It makes exchange of ideas more difficult – and exchange of ideas is what this profession is about. You have to pay for that with a lot of travel time and costs. The fact that we are located in two cities is not an ideal situation for me."
MICHAEL SPOLJARIC, PHANTOM:RESEARCH-FOUNDATION: "You meet more people: Steve Johnston [Spoljaric's partner in Phantom Research] is in London and I am in America. That already doubles the amount of people to meet."
MARCO FIEDLER, VIER5: "[One of the advantages is] having the time to read in the train as you travel from one country to the next."

Graphic design is about communication, do designers need to take care not to isolate themselves from the street and their urban environment?
STEFAN YANKU: "Design responds to the environment – it is a dialogue. It is not possible to isolate oneself. Not only cities, even the quietness of the mountains can have a strong influence on creative work. Design reflects the thoughts of the designer as well as his cultural background and his environment."
MARCO FIEDLER, VIER5: "Yes and no, as a designer one shouldn't lose one's relationship with the outside, but one shouldn't lose the one to the inside either. I think there are phases when one needs to go out and when one needs to be alone. I am also certain that this is the same for other professions. We all have the same systems that we use – only the results are different."

Does it help being a foreigner in a city location e.g. Swedes in New York or Germans in Portugal? Does it give you a quirky edge or a different perspective?

STEFAN YANKU: "Of course it's highly inspiring to experience a different environment. Many aspects of one's own environment are overlooked. Trips to foreign countries may even make one's own home more intelligible and heighten the senses."
DAG HENNING BRANDSAETER: "From personal experience, when I first left Norway to study at Hyper Island in Sweden it was a great learning experience, even though it is a neighbouring country. It's a bit like starting from scratch. When I later moved to New York I felt the same thing all over again. It's an overwhelming feeling of new impulses and contrasts which is nothing but pure inspiration."
FLORIAN PFEFFER, JUNG + PFEFFER: "Over the past five years I have worked in Germany, The Netherlands, Lebanon and the USA. The most important insight that I could gain from this is that things are done completely different in different places and they are all valid."

How has your virtual location – having a home base in hyperspace – effected life as a designer?
JORK ANDRÉ DIETER: "It doesn't matter where I am, I can be anywhere, all I need is my laptop and a high-speed Internet connection."
RILLA ALEXANDER, RINZEN: "I think the Internet has actually changed design enormously. When we first graduated (1994) we were in a very strict graphic design world. The only books we looked at were graphic design books, we had no way of really connecting with the rest of the world. We were working in our local areas and, of course, we knew what was happening elsewhere, but at least a year after it had actually happened. The Internet really opened everything up. It completely changed the boundaries. All of a sudden we could talk to people on the other side of the world who were our absolute heroes and find that they were human beings and were into what we were doing too. Also it meant that there was an outlet for all these things that people were doing. Instead of mucking around and doing this stuff and looking at it yourself, you could put it on the Web. That's where the whole art thing really went crazy because there were all these things that people were doing with no clients. They were doing stuff with a design language but it wasn't actually graphic design in the sense that there was no client and there was no message that was being communicated."

VIER5

LOCATION: Paris, France

PROFILE: Marco Fiedler and Achim Reichert studied together at the Hochschule für Gestaltung in Offenbach in Germany. While Reichert concentrated on typography and photography, Fiedler devoted his college years to sculpture and installation. They set up Vier5 in Frankfurt after graduation but abandoned their homeland for Paris in 2002. "We moved to Paris because there is a lot going on to do with fashion, which we were always interested in, and because there is great interest here in experimental design work. We were in Frankfurt for ten years, and after ten years you simply want to seek out new pastures and widen your own horizons – and Paris is a great city."

MISSION: "We see ourselves as a design office in the classical sense. That is, we are interested in the design and development of things. At the moment we work mainly in the areas of graphic design and typography. We have no philosophy, we reject that sort of thing; we are not an advertising agency. Philosophies are restrictive and often turn out to be devoid of content – they are not modern. We are led more from personal, fundamental principles based on modern, contemporary design and on the creation of new, self-contained images and the desire for artistic design. Our work is independent artistic work, it should be clear and not subject to compromise."

CLIENTS: "We see clients as partners that we work with, not as customers. We are currently working with the Centre d'Art Contemporain de Bretigny, an art space on the outskirts of Paris, doing "FAIRY TALE" and realising various artists' catalogue projects."

CAC

CLIENT: Centre d'Art Contemporain de Bretigny, France

BRIEF: Create a series of posters for exhibitions at this contemporary arts centre.

CONCEPT: "Right from the beginning we did not want to illustrate the work of the artists. We saw our task more as interpreting the work of the artists in our own way. Before we start such a project we examine the artists' work intensively, look at sketches and already completed projects and then we think about what it triggers off in us. We believe that modern art can be represented by modern graphic design, but it would be a mistake to think that a simple reproduction of modern art (on a poster for example) is also a representation. You need new images to represent an image and we intended to find these new images."

SOLUTION: "The result was a huge range of posters in different print variations. Everyone who visited the exhibition could take home a poster that was a unique artistic creation. Because of the large number of variations, the posters had the feeling of being unique."

LESSON: "Most important of all is respect for the work of others and the understanding of their work. Also, anyone who attempts to design 'simple' posters for an exhibition ought to be locked up because 'simple' in this instance usually means 'bad' and has more to do with lack of courage than restraint."

David Lamelas

CAC BRETIGNY

Exposition 'L'effet écran'
12 juin — 15 octobre 2004

Centre d'art contemporain de Brétigny
Espace Jules Verne,
Rue Henri Douard
91220 Brétigny s/Orge, France
Tel: (33) 01 60 85 20 76
Fax: (33) 01 60 85 04 28
info@cacbretigny.com
www.cacbretigny.com
fermeture annuelle du 9 août du 20 septembre

CAC
BRETIGNY

exposition: The Technocrat The Edutainer

Atelier Van Lieshout

exposition: Phalanstère

Saâdane Afif, Yves Bélorgey, Giasco
Bertoli, Mircea Cantor, Serge Comte, Lionel
Estève, Jens Haaning,
Lutz Huelle, David Lamelas, Mathieu
Mercier, Marie Moor & Laurent Chambert,
Roman Ondak,
Paola Pivi, Bojan Sarcevic, SFC 750,
Santiago Sierra, Amie Vigier & Franck
Apertet, Vier5, Wang Du,
Artur Zmijewski

12 octobre au 20 décembre 2003

Centre d'art contemporain
de Brétigny
Espace Jules Verne,
rue Henri Douard
91220 Brétigny-sur-Orge
Renseignements et accès:
Infoline 01 60 85 20 76
www.cacbretigny.com

FAIRY TALE

CLIENT: Self-generated fashion magazine project: Fairy Tale, Paris, France

BRIEF: "To develop a magazine that is completely different from any other in this fashion / art sector. The magazine is to be published twice yearly."

CONCEPT: "The idea is that all contributions will be commissioned in a kind of briefing from the contributors, so as to encourage a strong interaction between the magazine makers and the photographers, stylists and authors. This is to avoid the impression (as with so many magazines) that the photographers deliver their photo shoots as a prepackaged product."

SOLUTION: "A magazine of two halves; Each editor produces a single section, completely in black and white. Different cover versions, with different motifs and coloured typographic variations are created using screen-printing techniques. Thus each issue would have ten different covers. A new layout and typefaces will be developed for each issue. This will give individual issues, on the shelf, the effect of seeming to be one-offs."

LESSON: "That there is absolutely no reason whatsoever in design terms to make a magazine that looks just like all the others on the racks at the newsagent."

FT

NEW
BEAUTY

SURFACE

LOCATION: Frankfurt + Berlin, Germany

PROFILE: "Surface was founded in 1997. It has bases in Frankfurt and Berlin, with twelve employees and two directors (Markus Weisbeck and Ann Theobald). Our team consists of graphic design graduates, art historians, artists and organizers. In 2000 we founded our own art music label called 'whatness'. Surface's field of operations covers the design of texts and images for all kinds of media and products. The way in which we focus on the content and the product results in design that has not only a visual form, but also an editorial, curatorial and advisory one too."

MISSION: "Surface emphasises the conceptual translation of content and consciously dissociates itself from classical advertising. Contrary to classical advertising, we actively decided against the production of attractive, but empty 'shells' and superficial approaches to clients, personalities and products. Our approach never puts the visualisation in competition with the content, rather it translates and accentuates it. We try to bring advertising and campaigns back from being just about image to being about content again. In this sense, we have no 'mission'; our intent is about content, structures and principles."

CLIENTS: Ballett Frankfurt, Cocoon Event GmbH, Daimler Chrysler, Deutsche Guggenheim Berlin, Edition Olms, Zürich, EnOf, Rotterdam, Frankfurter Kunstverein, Frankfurt, Galerie Johann König, Berlin, Galerie Schipper und Krome, Hugo Boss AG, Institute of Contemporary Art, Boston, Jüdisches Museum, Frankfurt, K7 Records, Kostas Murkudis GmbH, Lukas and Sternberg, New York, Mille Plateaux, Frankfurt, Rhizome, New York, Schirn Kunsthalle Frankfurt, Verlag Birkhäuser, Verlag für Modern Kunst, Nuremberg, Verlag Hatje Cantz, Virgin Records.

ART FRANKFURT

CLIENT: Art Frankfurt, Messe Frankfurt GmbH, Germany

BRIEF: Design and develop an advertising campaign for Art Frankfurt – an art fair for 'young art'.

CONCEPT: "The need was for a new image for the Art Frankfurt that showed the fair as representing a broad range of art in a clear, elegant and honest way."

SOLUTION: "Heavily abstracted photos of contemporary artworks from the exhibitors formed the basis of collages, which were then cut out and put back together in a new format. The resulting images were modular variations, which could be recombined again and again. The resulting images were used for a poster series, adverts, postcards, tickets, stickers, catalogue, VIP tickets and more."

LESSON: "The desired effect really did occur; collectors, gallerists and visitors were all kept busy trying to guess which artworks the images originally came from."

art ɟɹnɟʞuɐɹɟ 2004

Young Arts Fair
Avantgarde, Modern, Edition

May 7 - 10
11 a.m. to 8 p.m., last day to 6 p.m.
Messe Frankfurt, Hall 1, City Entrance
www.artfrankfurt.de
Phone + 49 69 75 75 - 66 64

Messe
Frankfurt

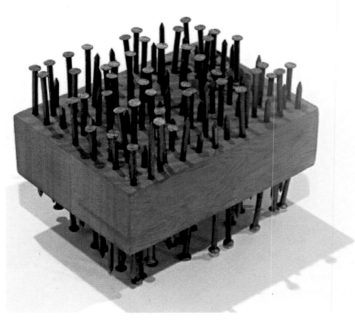

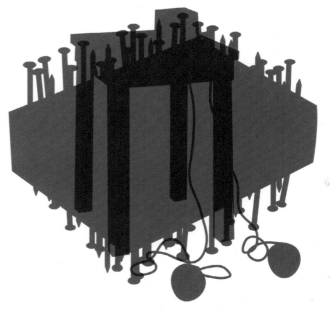

BALLETT FRANKFURT
DECREATION
VON WILLIAM FORSYTHE
3./4./5./6. SEPTEMBER 2003 BOCKENHEIMER DEPOT, 20 UHR
KARTEN: 069 / 13 40 400 UND AN ALLEN BEKANNTEN VORVERKAUFSSTELLEN
WWW.BALLETT-FRANKFURT.DE

BALLETT FRANKFURT
NEUPRODUKTION
VON WILLIAM FORSYTHE
16./17./18./22./24./26. APRIL 2004 OPERNHAUS AM WILLY-BRANDT-PLATZ 20 UHR
KARTEN: 069 / 13 40 400 UND AN ALLEN BEKANNTEN VORVERKAUFSSTELLEN
WWW.BALLETT-FRANKFURT.DE

BALLETT FRANKFURT

CLIENT: Ballett Frankfurt, Frankfurt am Main, Germany

BRIEF: Produce a campaign for the Ballett Frankfurt 2003–2004 season

CONCEPT: "Sculptural and mathematical elements of William Forsythe's choreography were combined with elements of movement photography. Harold Edgerton, the 20th-century pioneer of scientific photography, photographed movement as a series of stills, which produced a visualisation of movement as sequence. The sculptural sequence of the individually choreographed movements represented a retrospective view of Forsythe's work with the Ballett Frankfurt."

SOLUTION: "The idea of the 2003–2004 campaign was based on the idea of a Forsyth 'library' that attempted to fix his style and the resulting shapes as a sculptural archive. The images were made using stroboscopic photography."

LESSON: "Every photographic campaign only works in extremely close collaboration with the photographer and necessitates precise definitions to reach the required result. Of equal importance is the co-operation with the dancers, which gives the whole thing authenticity in the first place."

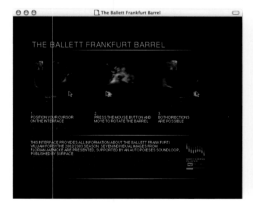

SOUND CHAMBERS

CLIENT: Sound Chambers, Fundacao Serralves, Porto, Portugal

BRIEF: Develop a sound sculpture with graphic, architectural and musical elements.

CONCEPT: "The main idea was the development of a tautological work that was both music and sculpture. A graphic notation made up of empty spaces from a plan of the park was transformed into music, by the musicians, using software analysis, and an architecture of negative interstices was created from the same elements."

SOLUTION: "Sound Chambers is a site-specific installation in the Museu Serralves park in Porto. The structure, whose shape is influenced by the geometrical configuration of the surrounding hedges, expands, pushes and splits the existing conditions of the park. It creates a system between the internal and external spaces and creates 'sound chambers'. Specially composed music, architecture and graphics take up the themes of the park and 77 different geometric elements arrange themselves into a new composition."

LESSON: "That it is possible to open doors creatively and to use translation methods to move from one medium to another and back again."

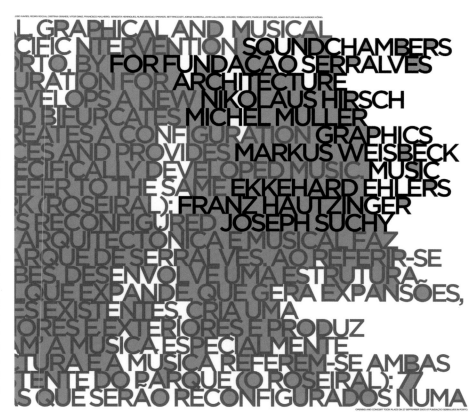

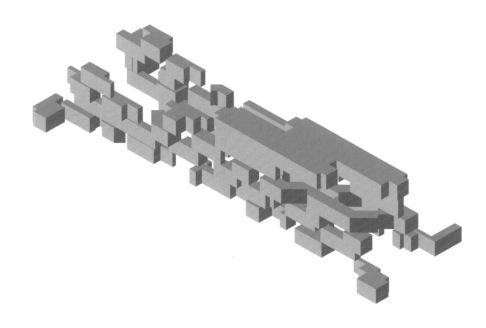

FRANÇOIS CHALET

LOCATION: Zurich, Switzerland

PROFILE: Chalet studied graphic design in Bern, Switzerland between 1991 and 1996. While studying he had a three-month internship at Nous Travaillons in Paris and a two-month internship at Moniteurs in Berlin. He went freelance after completing college and is based in Zurich.

MISSION: "My work consists of trying to create my own universe with inhabitants, houses, forms and its own vocabulary. I help to bring it to life through posters, animations, VJ-ing and other media. I want to offer my own personal view, or interpretation, of the world. I think that the more interpretations there are the more interesting the world is!"

CLIENTS: "I think that clients come to me because they know my work. Often they come because they have seen something and they want to have something similar. Yes I have a house style, but this style can change or be adapted to the client. But, if they do come to me then they will get a Chalet interpretation." Clients include; MTV Germany, MTV UK (MTV European Music Awards), Mitsubishi Japan, OP Vodka, dalbin.com, primalinea.com

LES FABRIQUES ORCHESTRALES

CLIENT: Fête de la Musique, Paris, France

BRIEF: "I was asked to take part in a competition to make a folding poster for the Fête de la Musique 2004 in Paris, advertising the main attraction, Les Fabriques Orchestrales. It was a collection of around eight music kiosks in the park with hip-hop, pop-rock, electronic music, singing, etc. There were four of us competing and each had a measly budget of 450 euros."

CONCEPT + SOLUTION: "I designed a character on the computer for each event, printed them out and cut them out of card. Then I created an audience, a cat, the typography as well. This all took about a week. Then I had to find a suitable patch of grass to set the whole scene up. The presentation was in Paris and I only had a day left to get the photo done for it. It was windy and a woman from New York, that I happened to have fallen in love with the day before, was also at the shoot which effected my concentration considerably. Also there was a whole bunch of little kids around having a lot of fun, which didn't exactly make things any easier. In the end we ran out of time and the light went. Lozza, the photographer, shot the picture, I printed out a plot of it and set off to Paris to present it to an eight member jury. A couple of days later, I heard that that two of us had been shortlisted and that I only had a chance of winning if a new design with more readable text could be presented to the jury in three days time. New text meant re-shooting the whole thing but I didn't hesitate for long. We found a new, slightly steeper, location where we could make the image a little more compact. The problem was, the sun was threatening to disappear behind a house. We didn't have time to think about another location though, so we set the whole thing up again (with readable text). Lozza rushed off into town to get a film, I set up as fast as I could (extreme concentration) and, oh horror, just as he got back the whole shadow of the house fell across the installation. Lozza had to go back to the studio to get his flash kit, set it all up and when it was all ready, the sun came back out from behind the house. So the second photo was done and tidied up in Photoshop. It was then sent to Paris as a PDF and Eric Dalbin, who had organised the whole admin side, handed it in to the jury. The rejection letter arrived a few days later.

LESSON: "It was brilliant fun and I'd do it again anyday."

GENEVIÈVE GAUCKLER

LOCATION: Paris, France

PROFILE: Gauckler was born in Lyon in 1967. She started her career designing album covers for F Communications and then went on to videos and animation. In 1999 she moved to London, where she joined the Swedish Internet start-up Boo.com and also worked with Me Company, concentrating more on interactive design. She now works in France as an independent graphic designer and is a member of the Pleix group of musicians, 3D artists and designers.

MISSION: Gauckler's realm is the "magical" side of graphics software. She occupies worlds defined by vector graphics, Photoshop and After Effects. Her output covers a broad spectrum from CD covers and videos to posters, web design and animation. Her distinctive trademarks are her digital mandalas – digital image collages of apparent complexity and witty symmetry.

CLIENTS: Art Grandeur Nature exhibition, Lab, Bleip, Yakuta, Mass Appeal.

POSTERS IN THE PARK

CLIENT: Département de la Seine-Sant-Denis, France

BRIEF: A group of eight artists was asked to each design five posters to be displayed in a park in a northern Paris suburb. Gauckler was one of these artists.

CONCEPT: Because of the natural setting, Gauckler thought it would be interesting to design her own abstract interpretation of trees. The commission was challenging because, although she likes to create something completely different for each project she works on, she found a brief with no constraints to be a little unnerving.

SOLUTION: Gauckler used collages made from photographs she had taken in the USA a few months earlier to create five giant images somewhere between trees, Rorschach tests and mandalas.

LESSON: "I learned that I can do art stuff."

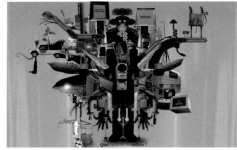

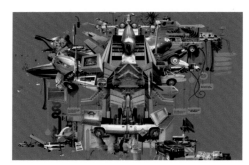

DOUBLE STANDARDS

LOCATION: Berlin, Germany

PROFILE: Double Standards was founded by Chris Rehberger in 2002 after he split from the Standard Rad design studio that he co-founded in Frankfurt and Berlin. The studio currently comprises eight people and includes graphic designers, product designers, film and post-production specialists and a corporate design consultant.

MISSION: "Design is more or less about giving an idea a logical form. We fight for the consequences of straightforward ideas without any blasphemous or lame compromise. Communication consists of strong statements. Design does fight. Good design lacks of democratic consensus. Our work is aware, honest and authentic – never touched by hype."

CLIENTS: Neue National Galerie, Berlin; Design Plus Messe, Frankfurt; Tommy Hilfiger, Amsterdam; Olafur Eliasson /Tate Modern, London; Galleria Gió Marconi, Milan; Deutsches Hygene Museum, Dresden; Bl_nks fashion shop, Berlin; Schirn Kunsthalle, Frankfurt; LAB01.

HAU

CLIENT: Hebbel am Ufer Theatre, Berlin, Germany

BRIEF: Produce a logo, campaign and corporate identity to re-launch a well-known Berlin theatre for experimental performing arts and attract a new audience.

CONCEPT: H.A.U. is an abbreviation of the theatre's name and also means "hit" or "punch" in German. As an interpretation of this word association, Double Standards and the photographer Monika Rehberger came up with this visual campaign. The boxers featured are young people, hot and sweaty, with black eyes after a fight. They appear tired yet satisfied. The analogy seems to be that a trip to the Hebbel is hard work but a worthwhile experience.

SOLUTION: The boxer concept and accompanying graphic design was applied to the whole corporate design of the theatre from Internet presence to posters, programmes, letterheads and house signage.

LESSON: The client identified and adapted to the idea in an instant proving that "theatre people" are nowhere near as difficult and complicated as the Double Standards team were expecting them to be.

SPIELZEITBEGINN AM 31.10. HALLESCHES UFER 32
HEBBEL AM UFER KREUZBERG 61
TEL. 030-259004-0
WWW.HEBBEL-AM-UFER.DE

HAU
DREI

GÜNTER EDER

LOCATION: Vienna, Austria

PROFILE: "I graduated from the HTL für Kunst und Design (Ortweinschule) in Graz, Austria in 1991. From 1992 onwards, I worked as an art director in various advertising agencies and graphic design studios until I started my own business in 2000."

MISSION: "I interpret graphic design in an extended way: It is not just about the pure form or the structure of an object, there are other processes behind what is visible. My work comprises a lot of research, communication, development of concepts and typography, as well as corporate and editorial design. Right now I am working in collaboration with a partner in a two-man-office, but we are connected to an open network of other studios working in the field of design or related areas, such as architecture, media design and cultural management. Concerning my work, I think that it should be able to adjust to the specific desires and demands of each client. Also, each product has its own specific qualities and thus requires a different approach. Generally speaking, I think that the best results are to be obtained when the product inspires me or when I am somehow challenged by the job."

CLIENTS: A1 Mobilkom Austria, ATV-Plus Privat TV, Dazed&Confused, dietheater, EOOS Design GmbH, Gasteiner Mineralwasser, Künstlerhaus Wien, MuseumsQuartier, Schauspielhaus Wien, Universität für angewandter Kunst (Wien), Wien Museum.

SCHAUSPIELHAUS WIEN

CLIENT: Schauspielhaus (Theatre), Vienna, Austria

BRIEF: Come up with a logo, corporate design, poster and flyer.

CONCEPT: This was a collaborative project with the agency Jung von Matt Donau, Günter Eder and Andreas Putz as creative directors, photography from Jork Weismann, Paint Box by Albert Winkler, graphics by Stefanie Putz and consultancy from Josef König and Caroline Floh. The concept was to find a graphic interpretation for the mood and sentiments of the theatrical performances.

SOLUTION: The image of the snake became both logo and totem for the theatre. The main — and theoretically quite simple — idea was to create images of people/creatures that don't really exist; examples of "human metamorphosis" reflecting the transition between actor and character, between reality, suspension of belief and the fantasy that is theatre.

LESSON: "Digital retouching."

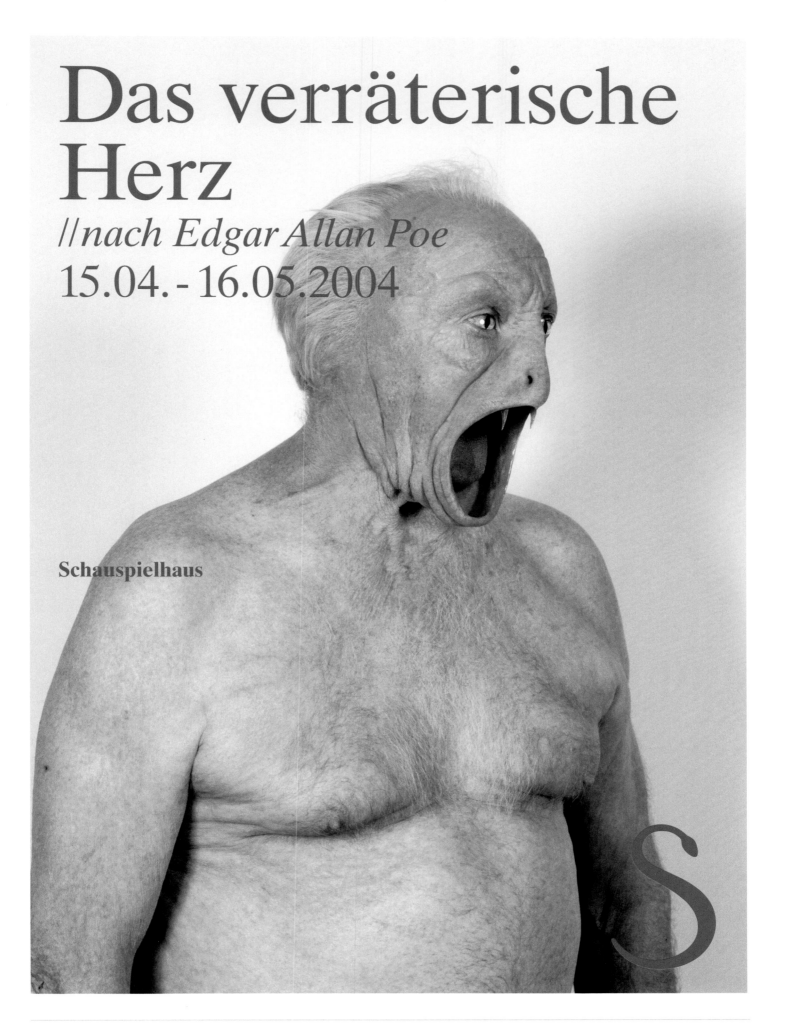

Das verräterische
Herz
//nach Edgar Allan Poe
15.04. - 16.05.2004

Schauspielhaus

4

Co-operation

Loners and Collectives

"I don't believe in design collectives, or more precisely, I could never see myself opening a design studio. The idea of multiplying my skills and producing graphic design/art direction on a larger scale does not interest me at all. Employing a team of people is the least of my desires."
KASIA KORCZAK

Designers tend to attach particular value to their personal freedom. The creative process is often highly individual which can make accommodating standard office practices a little tricky. A few can barely even tolerate the compromises involved in working to a brief. Although working solo entails nothing like the isolation involved in the pre-Internet days, confirmed lone wolves still exist: Martin Woodtli, François Chalet, Dipesh Pandya and Kasia Korczak for example. That is not to say that they are not happy to work with others on a project of interest but for them the smallest unit is generally the most flexible and therefore most comfortable. Other designers love to collaborate for short periods of time on particular projects but are metaphorically off saddling their horse and heading out of town again as soon as the task is completed. Thus in classic hired gun style, Jork Andre Dieter calls himself a "team player that works alone"; Katja Gretzinger lets the job decide and takes a relatively neutral stance: "I work in teams or alone – it depends on the project" and other freelancers like Klaus Haapaniemi and Sophie Toporkoff say much the same.

Another category seems to be those who cherish their individuality, yet hate to be alone and thus seek out other like-minded collaborators to form groups with whom they are commercially bound to a greater or lesser extent. Collaborations range from the inseparable couple with added love interest such as Antoine + Manuel, through the classic partnership-turned-company like Dixonbaxi, to organisations comprising a multitude of directors or egalitarian collectives and even the odd proto-totalitarian regime. For Stefan Yanku it is the feedback that comes from working with others that is of greatest value. "I like to work in interdisciplinary teams like web designer and programmer for example. The project also gets drive and inspiration from this. Everyone does what he can do best, the project proceeds and the members can learn a lot from each other. I think a team can only win: maybe a pitch gets lost, but a strong team discusses the reasons for its failure and is strengthened by its conclusions."

One of the most interesting set-ups is that of Rinzen in Australia. Founder member Rilla Alexander describes her company as a "collaborative". It is a group of five designers who are all directors, and no employees. She says they only take on work that they can manage themselves without using extra staff; they don't put their individual names to projects but always credit work to "Rinzen". She also says that when she and her husband Steve discussed initiating the group, many advised them against this egalitarian model; "But we believe very strongly that you can't get the best creative work out of people unless they truly believe in it and it is theirs, otherwise you are employing people, putting them in a situation where there's always tensions and so when they know everything and have all the client contacts they disappear! Which is basically what I did in every job I ever had. So the best employees are also the worst employees because they are not going to stick around. Within Rinzen, we were all really good friends from the beginning and I felt that it was really important that we were all equal."

Other designers work in organisations that seem far less tight-knit; sometimes a particular attitude, approach or style of working can be enough to cement together a group over significant distances. Base, for example, has 32 members of staff and four directors divided between Belgium, Barcelona, New York and Madrid, yet it still maintains a strong sense of company identity. Even the name "Base" implies the existence of one central hub and since that hub is clearly not geographical, then it must have something to do with ideology. The Phantom Research Foundation too is based in the USA and UK and calls itself "an artists', musicians' and designers' collective". ITF Grafik Design comprises four individuals in three German cities united by their name, which stands for, "In True Friendship". But despite the descriptive terminology used by these groups, they rarely seem to be governed by any political or philosophical dogma. Whether bound together as directors and staff, partners or comrades, the reasons for being a group seem to have more to do with "feel good factors" than ideological manifestoes; ITF's unifying principle is "the friendship that connects the four of us and the great respect we have for each other's work", and Stephen Johnston and Michael Spoljaric say they created Phantom Research Foundation as an environment in which "to be playful and not take ourselves too seriously".

These loose collective or collaborative models also seem to have distinct advantages when it comes to adaptability and creative experimentation. Alexander says that part of Rinzen's manifesto — if they had one — would remind them to be flexible and that the key to their success is co-operation with one another. "We didn't start Rinzen for 'business' reasons, but because we really enjoyed collaborating with each other, we could see so many possibili-

ties for what we could do together and knew we had different strong points, so that helped us to create something different from what we would have done alone. As long as this is still happening, then we are doing fine."

Co-operation facilitates flexibility when designers function as discrete units that are not constantly fixed in terms of the colleagues they work with, or the medium that they work in, and the tendency seems to be to say that this is what promotes creativity. Stefan Yanku again: "I believe in the kind of teamwork that respects the goals of the projects and the individual members". This flexible co-operation can also be seen in the relationship between designers and clients, a co-operation that can be as simple as sharing a workspace, as in the case of State and their main client onedotzero. Co-operation on a slightly larger scale and more complex level can be seen with the fashion company Diesel. Diesel makes a point of collaborating with a large number of exterior creatives to help maintain a strong cutting-edge image in the highly volatile visual world of fashion. Bob Shevlin, Head of the New Media department at Diesel describes how this works. "Diesel has all the components of a good-sized advertising agency...There is this kind of loose group inside Diesel which is the creative team run by a small number of people with a staff of maybe 60 (clothing designers, graphic designers, merchandising designers, web designers etc.). They all work in one building separate from the Diesel headquarters. And we also work with new freelance creatives and agencies every season on different projects."

Of course, this is still a client / supplier relationship and Diesel, like all clients, are still — strictly speaking — enhancing their own profile by tapping into the creative talent of others, but the approach still has a mood of a collaboration

or co-operation and Diesel take great pains to emphasise the freedom that they give their designers, and that projects often arise from a sort of mutual cross-fertilisation. Take, for example, the Lost Paradise animation project (see pages 176-7) that Shevlin commissioned from Lobo. "Some of the talent-scouting that Diesel does is virtual: I think the first contact we had with Lobo for example was through a website. We wanted to do a creative execution on our website where we invited around 15 different motion graphic people to interpret one of our seasonal advertising themes — emotions. There weren't any real rules to this thing. If we find people to work on that kind of basis we choose them because we think they've got something to say so we don't want to give them strict parameters. Then Lobo turned in something that was really good and we liked it. So we got the organisers of the Offfestival in Barcelona (that we were sponsoring) to invite Mateus over to speak at the conference and I met him there and was so impressed with him that I asked him to come over to the office in Italy to show him the new clothing collection. An entire project grew out of this visit, which resulted in the Lost Paradise animation pieces, which ended up being a TV commercial."

It almost goes without saying that a key component of all this co-operation is, of course, the way the Internet has opened up channels of immediate communication. Groups of individuals that are scattered all over the globe can complete sections of projects for, or with, or about each other without ever meeting up. Given a common language, compatible software, a broadband connection and a sense of creative affinity it seems that there are ways of working with others out there that designers and their clients are only just beginning to touch upon.

LUST

LOCATION: The Hague, The Netherlands

PROFILE: The name LUST came from the graduation projects of founders Thomas Castro and Jeroen Barendsee. The company was formed in 1996 with the support of an arts grant from the Netherlands Foundation for the Visual Arts and Design. Dimitri Nieuwenhuizen joined as a partner in 1999. Today it is a small studio of four to five designers with between four and six interns per year. They say their work is composed of around 40% interactive and time-based media, 40% traditional and printed media, 10% font design and 10% self-initiated projects.

MISSION: "Our design philosophy revolves around process-based design, coincidence, the degradation of form and content, form-follows-process, and contextuality versus textuality. Topics include typography, graphic design, typography, abstract cartography, mapping, random mistake-ism, fonts, type design, multimedia, and interactive web design."

CLIENTS: "Lust works for architects and city planners, publishers, music groups, galleries, fine art institutions and various other small cultural entities as well as some larger institutions, such as Dutch ministries, municipalities and national museums. The biggest project we have worked on so far is the Digital Depot project for Museum Bojimans van Beuningen in Rotterdam."

HOEK VAN HOLLAND

CLIENT: Rotterdam 2001, Cultural Capital of Europe, The Netherlands

BRIEF: To highlight the Hook of Holland as the beach and water recreation area of Rotterdam during the Rotterdam 2001, Cultural Capital year.

CONCEPT: To produce a map and temporary installations, together with the urbanist Jan de Graaf, that revealed the many facets of the Hook of Holland: historic, economic, industrial, residential, maritime, recreational etc.

SOLUTION: A two-metre-wide map was needed to accommodate all the information. A folding system was devised that eliminated the need for constantly folding and refolding the map to see particular sections. A special projection of the world was developed that placed the Hook of

Holland in the middle of the map. On the reverse side is the tidal and lunar information for the area for a complete year. A full moon is represented in solid blue and a new moon in 10% blue with all the gradations in between. The result is a symbolisation of the ebb and flow of the tides. Site-specific art installations were combined with the map project so that visitors could find them by using it. The map was a tool for the festival but it was also an investigation into the possibilities that maps offer while pushing the boundaries of cartographic conventions.

LESSON: "How one project can be formed from several different projects in such a way that makes the individual elements stronger."

De nieuwe kaart van

HOEK VAN HOLLAND

Hotel
Oskar
Echo
Kilo
Victor
Alpha
November
Hotel
Oscar
Lima
Lima
Alpha
November
Delta

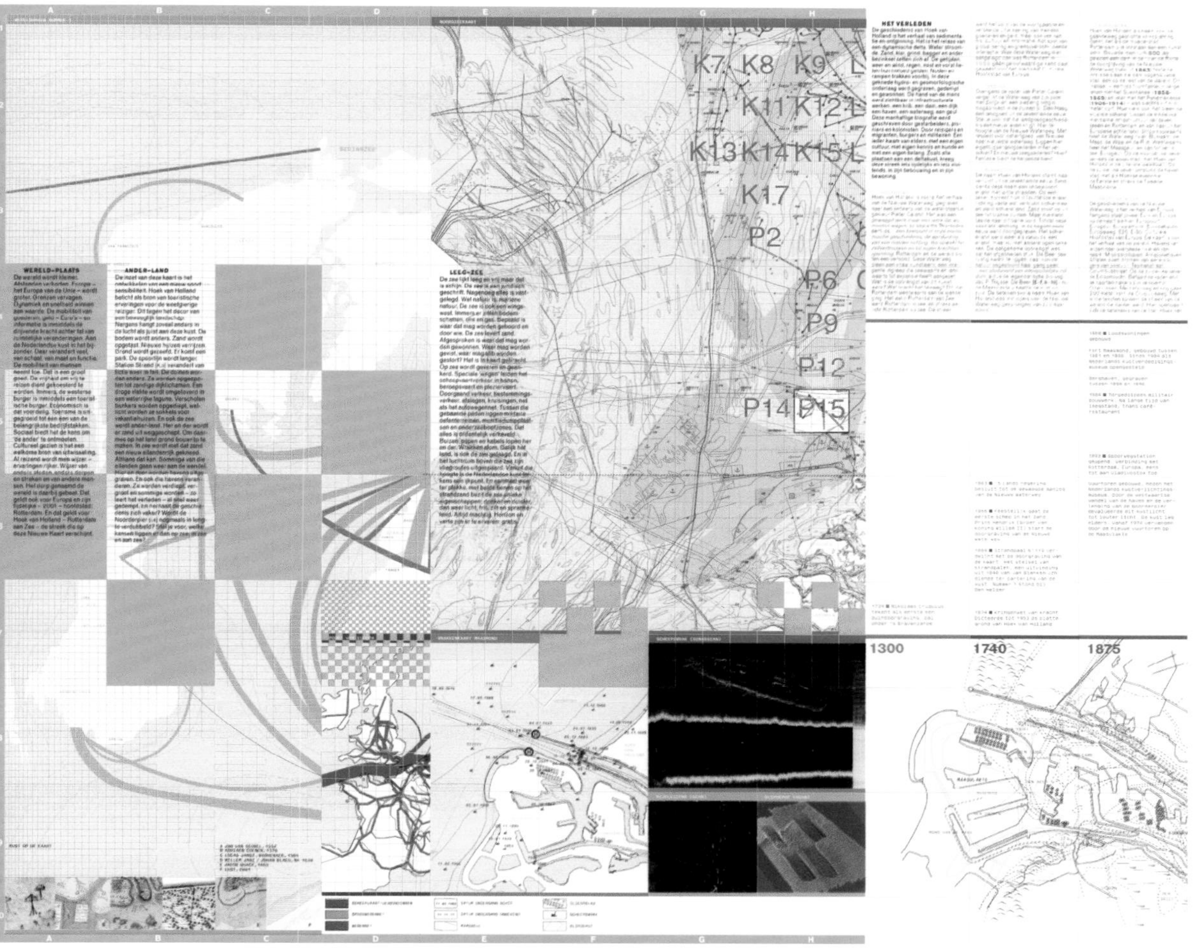

WERELD-PLAATS

ANDER-LAND

LEEG-ZEE

HET VERLEDEN

HET VERSCHIET

1300   1740   1875

1955   1970   **2001 >**

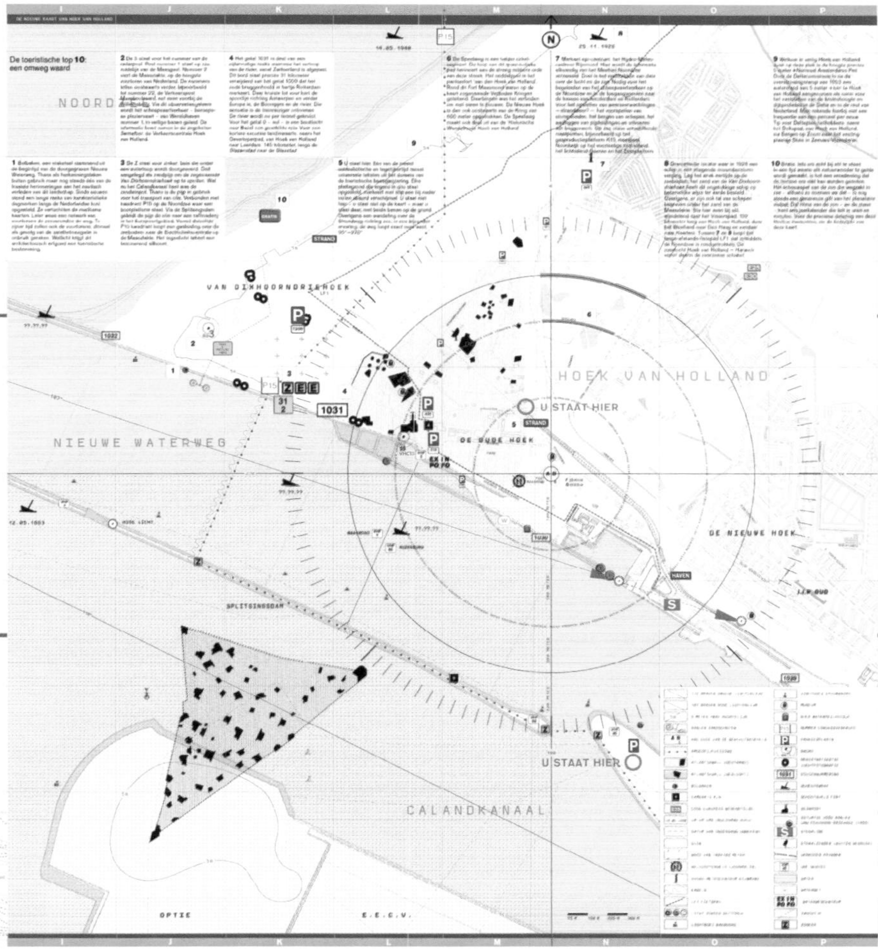

De toeristische top 10:
een omweg waard

NOORDZEE

VAN DIXHOORNDRIEHOEK

HOEK VAN HOLLAND

NIEUWE WATERWEG

U STAAT HIER

DE OUDE HOEK

DE NIEUWE HOEK

CALANDKANAAL

SPLITSINGSDAM

U STAAT HIER

OPTIE   E.E.C.V.

ZEE

NORTH SEA

CLIENT: Self-initiated project, together with Jan de Graaf and Steven van Schuppen

BRIEF: "To investigate whether there is such a thing as 'North Sea culture' using cartograohy as a starting point."

CONCEPT: "Even at the beginning of the project it was clear that there were lots of layers of information that needed to be combined in a clever way. We didn't want the sea to be just a blue surface on the map, but a world in its own right, with a history and a future. By using a matrix to create 440 maps we showed that there is an enormous amount of information about the North Sea and how one is manipulated by the way in which it is depicted."

SOLUTION: "The result was a book and a map. The book is an extension of the map; twenty-one essays describe twenty-one combinations of maps, leaving room for interpretation of the other 420 maps."

LESSON: "The challenge was how to make complicated information accessible to a wider audience, not by making the information easier to understand, but by putting different layers of understanding into the project."

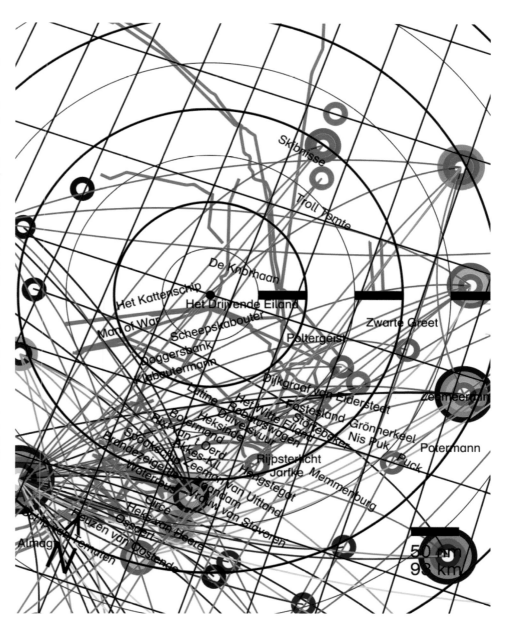

UNFOLDED

LOCATION: Zurich, Switzerland

PROFILE: "We do art, art direction, graphics and design: analog and digital, time-based and time-less, and most importantly interactive, no matter whether for print or digital. We come from different backgrounds such as fine art, graphics and design, new media and teaching." unfolded's founding members, Nadia Gisler and Friedrich-Wilhelm Graf first started to work together in 2001. "We figured out that we like working together and that we complement each other perfectly. Officially we founded unfolded in the winter of 2003, to become more serious in business-terms. For particular projects, we like to work with our wonderfully patient freelance crew of photographers, media artists, programmers, etc."

MISSION: "A passion, for work, process and output. A love of details and the side stories yet with eyes on the big picture. Our thinking and developing happens from scratch; every project is a kind of blank canvas. Our aim is to develop the best solution for each project and we will fight for the better way instead of giving in to the easy solution."

CLIENTS: Theaterblut, Sound-Inspiration, Tommy Fjordside, Olivier Blaser, Plan B, composer Peter Cadisch, Knowbotic Research.

THEATERBLUT

CLIENT: Schweizerischer Bühnenverband (SVB: Swiss Stage Association) together with the Hochschule Musik und Theater (HMT: Music and Theatre College) and Hochschule für Gestaltung und Kunst Zürich (HGKZ: Zurich College of Art and Design)

BRIEF: Originally the SVB commissioned an interactive CD-Rom to introduce young people to the practical and career dimensions of theatre.

CONCEPT: As unfolded began to tackle the project, it became clear that what was really needed was not a CD-Rom, but a complete, flexible and expandable system based around a website. The client agreed to their suggestion on the condition that the original budget and timeframe were adhered to.

SOLUTION: Interaction was of primary importance to the designers; they came up with an animated Flash website crammed with detail and an intuitive navigation world. In a similar manner, theaterblut 04, the non-virtual print version of the season programme, took the form of a do-it-yourself kit containing diary, calendar, notepad, stickers, postcards and key ring for each individual to build, plan and document their own theatre season of visits and dates.

LESSON: "It was a huge relief when all the puzzle pieces were finally finished and we could see that this was a work that functioned within itself and had depth. The tension that built up to this point (as well as lack of sleep) was almost unbearable. The project gave us self-confidence. We now have the courage to take on big projects and to trust in our abilities."

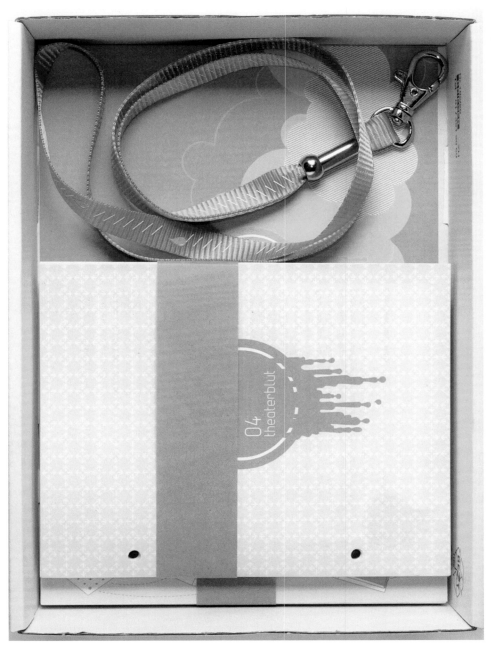

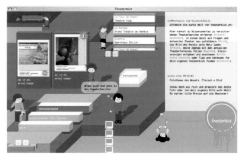

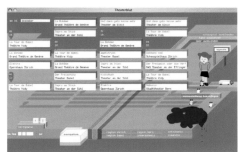

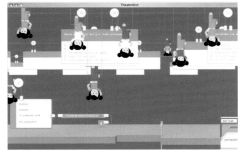

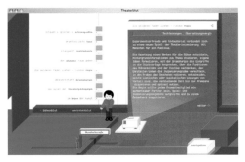

BRANDIGLOO™

LOCATION: Hamburg, Germany

PROFILE: Daniel Goddemeyer founded his own freelance business, BrandIgloo™, in 2003 for the development and distribution of creative software products and to market his Secret Diary™ web project. He studied at the Hochschule für Gestaltung in Offenbach am Main, Germany and graduated in 1999. Because, as he says, "dealing with digital media was relatively new at that time", he feels he learned the most about design and programming by working for FORK Unstable Media in Frankfurt and then Futurefarmers in San Francisco until 2002.

MISSION: Goddemeyer's main fields are graphic design and developing concepts and ideas for the web. He usually works together with a loose team of freelancers on individual projects: "It is useful having a group of people that you can count on and know the quality of their work. Also, larger jobs can be done together with a well-rehearsed team of project managers, programmers and additional designers."

CLIENTS: With work for FORK and Futurefarmers and as a freelancer, clients have included; Davidoff Cigarettes, Nivea, Greenpeace, Gruner and Jahr and Universal Music, among others.

SECRETDIARY™

THE CLIENT: "There was no client to begin with."

THE BRIEF: "The goal of the SecretDiary™ project was to make an online diary for just two people that could be sold in a shop as a real package."

THE CONCEPT: The concept arose from Goddemeyer's own experience of trying to maintain a long-distance relationship across the Atlantic. He wanted to develop a faster alternative to the traditional love letter that avoided the impersonal coldness of email.

THE SOLUTION: "Since the SecretDiary™ was intended to be a gift from one person to a special other, it was important that it had this haptic touch rather than just giving a digital code via email." The product took shape as a software package for a colourful, 3-D online space where correspondents can exchange virtual gifts and billets doux. There is the additional option of receiving a personal, bound hardcopy of the letters in book form.

THE RESULT: The project has now gone into mass production. "By having 'real packaging', the SecretDiary™ reaches a lot of people that have never or very seldom been in contact with web design and online communication."

LESSONS LEARNED: "The SecretDiary™ is my first product /project that was self-initiated and carried out from the first rough idea to the marketplace without having a client or investor. Besides all the technical and design stuff, I learned a lot about how difficult it can be to start your own company. I also learned a lot about project management, co-ordinating a lot of different people and keeping people motivated over a long period, without being able to pay them a lot of money. This wasn't always easy, but to grow, develop and produce your own idea is a very unique and interesting learning experience."

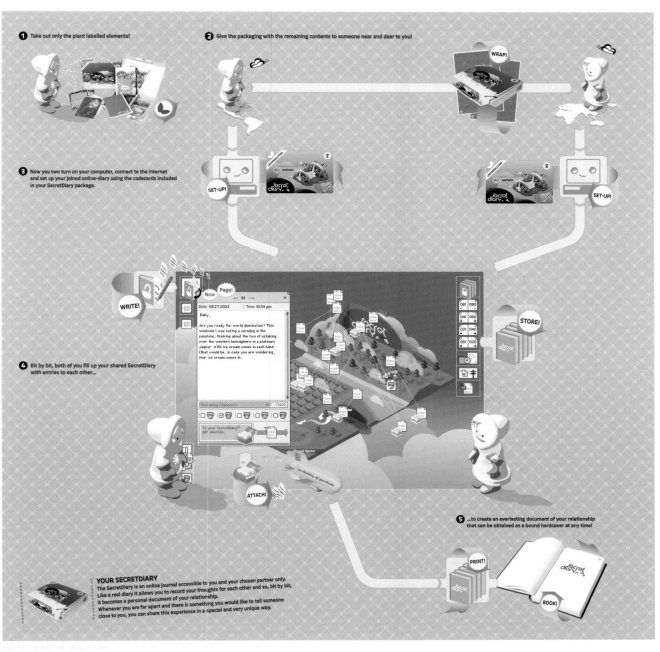

1 Take out only the plant labelled elements!

2 Give the packaging with the remaining contents to someone near and dear to you!

WRAP!

SET-UP!

SET-UP!

3 Now you two turn on your computer, connect to the internet and set up your joined online-diary using the codecards included in your SecretDiary package.

WRITE!

STORE!

New Page!

Date: 09.27.2003 | Time: 10:34 pm

Baby,

Are you ready for world domination? This weekend I was eating a corndog in the sunshine, thinking about the two of us taking over the western hemisphere in a platinum Jaguar. With ice cream cones in each hand (that would be, in case you are wondering, four ice cream cones in...

Remaining Characters

To your SecretDiary™ gift selection...

4 Bit by bit, both of you fill up your shared SecretDiary with entries to each other...

ATTACH!

5 ...to create an everlasting document of your relationship that can be obtained as a bound hardcover at any time!

PRINT!

BOOK!

YOUR SECRETDIARY
The SecretDiary is an online journal accessible to you and your chosen partner only.
Like a real diary it allows you to record your thoughts for each other and so, bit by bit,
it becomes a personal document of your relationship.
Whenever you are far apart and there is something you would like to tell someone
close to you, you can share this experience in a special and very unique way.

KASIA
KORCZAK

LOCATION: London, UK

PROFILE: Kasia Korczak was born and grew up in Poland then moved to London to study when she was 19. "I am a graphic designer and art director working across a wide range of creative disciplines from magazines to print, web design, motion graphics and inter-active design. I have been freelance for the last two-and-a-half years with a range of cli-ents in different countries. I studied Fine Art at the London Guildhall University between 1996 and 2000. While studying, I collaborated with an arts collective where I had my first proper design experience, but essentially I am a self-taught graphic designer. I never did an internship, but worked full-time as a graphic designer for agencies in London and Paris and decided to go independent in Paris in Spring 2002."

MISSION: "I don't believe in design collectives, or more precisely, I could never see myself opening a design studio. The idea of multiply-ing my skills and producing graphic design and art direction on a larger scale does not interest me at all. Employing a team of people is the least of my desires. Of course, having said that, I often work with Payam Shafifi and we do, in the end, tend to search for people with whom we work best, so when we find them we are reluctant to let them go. Our collaboration is very different from the usual set-up between design partners. There is always a new person that you can involve to make the job and the whole experience a lot better. I have been lucky enough to see some of my clients become my collaborators."

CLIENTS: Clients vary from fashion to cor-porate as well as many art-based, non-com-mercial projects: English National Ballet, UK; K2, Austria; Woda, Poland; K+P=WNM, France; Insead Business School, France; Alan Clarke, London; Bruise, Ltd., UK; L'Oréal, France; Nike, France; Cross Magazine, Italy; Mother, UK; VERRI, Italy; Elegant Touch, UK; La Pac, France.

LA PAC

CLIENT: La Pac, Paris, France

BRIEF: La Pac is the Grand Dame of the Parisian film and commercial production scene. It has been around for over 30 years and has over 60 Lion awards from Cannes including the Palme d'Or and the Grand Prix to its credit. The com-pany was nevertheless in need of a facelift and the brief was to rebrand and update the old company image to a newer and more relevant one, but to do so in a way that was appropriate to La Pac's particular history.

CONCEPT: "The main idea was based on the class system and the 'establishment' – a concept that was quiet alien to me since I grew up in a com-munist society – but nevertheless a very excit-ing subject. La Pac is the 'establishment', this is what they represent, but they also want to reap the benefits of being 'establishment' without appearing to rest on their laurels. I had noticed, whilst having lunch at the Parc Monceau, in La Pac's neighbourhood, a tradition that had again become popular with a younger generation of upper class women was the phenomenon of the small dog as accessory. It is an idea of luxury and establishment that had crossed over into another realm: it is aspirational and no longer looks out of date. So we used scenes of young socialite as opposed to an older lady as a back-drop for a multi-platform identity with the exist-ing logo."

SOLUTION: "We produced a scaleable website that could be updated by La Pac's staff without an in-depth knowledge of programming, and an identity that runs throughout their promotional material from DVD labels to business cards".

LESSON: "The main thing I realised working on this job is that you should always propose to the client much more than you think they will accept. Then it is easier to strip down an idea than to regret not having pushed it in the direction you wanted to go."

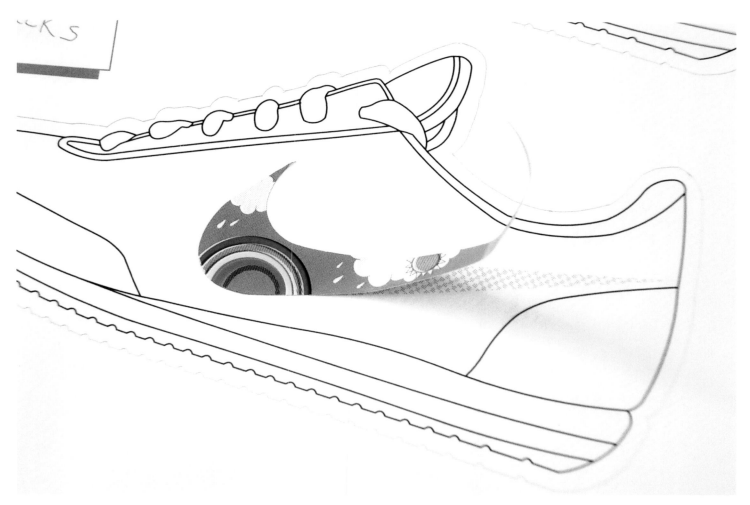

NIKE INFINITY

CLIENT: Nike, France

BRIEF: "To produce something which not only shows the concept for the new product, but also encourages a similar, playful, collective effect."

CONCEPT: "The client's request and the initial idea was to produce a booklet of some sort. But after getting to know the project, I realised that a booklet would not have the playful elements that the project required. So I decided to produce a swoosh sticker poster which enables you to play around and stick swooshes on the shoes or anywhere else in fact."

SOLUTION: "An A0-sized poster was produced, make entirely of sticky paper and featuring over 60 different swooshes from the 'Roy Lichtenstein' to the 'UN' swoosh. The swooshes were each 'kiss-cut', allowing fans to remove them one by one and try them on their shoes."

LESSON: "The best element in working on this job was the collaborative aspect. Working with a copywriter and an artist added a new dimension to the project, as well as new communication challenges."

FOUR23

LOCATION: Manchester, UK

PROFILE: Four23 calls itself a "special projects studio". "Our multi-disciplinary structure enables us to work across a broad range of media including graphic design, art installation, event management, interactive media, and the moving image."

MISSION: Four23 practice what they call "convergent design": "The new digital technologies have changed all our customers' lives; it's the emperor's new lines of communication not the emperor's new clothes. Restricting a good idea to one specific medium no longer makes sense – not to us anyway. Through interdisciplinary design, informed by research, we build relationships between our clients, their audience and the future success of their companies – whatever the medium. We have developed a six-stage methodology: question; define; structure; design; produce; evaluate. It's a system that works for us but we're not bound by it. Instead we see it as a series of key milestones to help us, and our clients, keep in check."

CLIENTS: Adidas, Rocco Forte Hotels, Ninja Tunes, Virgin Records, Manchester Art Gallery, NATEC, GM Connexions, Media Travel, Marketing Manchester, nmp, British Council, Urbis, CIDS, Royal College of Art, Elemental Arts, NWDA.

ADIDAS STORE LAUNCH

CLIENT: Adidas, Area North, UK

BRIEF: To create a marketing campaign for the launch and promotion of the first Adidas Originals Store in the UK in the Triangle shopping centre, Manchester.

CONCEPT: To make a campaign that was varied and unobtrusive yet effective. The idea was one of "assisted discovery", seemingly mysterious and somewhat subversive – "something that people came across rather than it being in your face".

SOLUTION: A variety of projects were used to promote the store: a "wallpaper art" campaign on billboards across the north of England, A2 foldout magazine inserts, a launch party with a Feng Shui plant installation ceremony and a giant, truck-sized Adidas shoe box placed in various peripheral urban locations. The public's interaction with this art cum product placement was filmed and shown as a three-hour film projected onto the walls of the new shop at the opening. During construction of the shop site, Four23's in-house artist Debbie Goldsmith also undertook a seven-day painting project on the surrounding hoardings.

LESSON: "Time isn't everything."

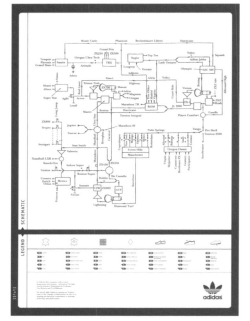

SATOSHI MATSUZAWA

LOCATION: Tokyo, Japan

PROFILE: "I have never studied design or illustration. I usually work alone, but for a big project like 'Edwin', I worked as part of a team with the production company. If I am working on an advertising project based on graphic design, then I usually work with a graphic designer. I mainly do illustration for the music industry (album covers etc.), and for the fashion industry. My work is based on illustration but sometimes I work on web design and graphic design."

MISSION: "I think my illustration style is very contemporary but contains 1960s and 1970s action movie elements. My illustration work also gives a feeling of music. My whole output is based on music – especially soul and jazz."

CLIENTS: "K-SWISS, J-WAVE (radio), TBS (broadcasting), asics, SHIBUYA109 (department store), and lots of record labels, both Japanese and overseas."

EDWIN JEANS

CLIENT: Edwin Company Limited, Japan

BRIEF: To stimulate the younger generation's interest in Edwin Jeans; to make the most of the jeans' characteristics; to reach kids aged between 10 and 20.

CONCEPT: "To emphasise the characteristics of the jeans, I developed seven illustrated characters with their own scenes and backgrounds."

SOLUTION: The resulting figures mean that the product can be advertised over and over again with the various characters in various different settings; "For example, for the TV commercial, we worked together to find a way to make the characters move and we discussed the sound and the facial expressions."

LESSON: "I learned a new method of production and representation that goes beyond illustration. I appreciated the solidarity of working with a production team from different industries, because this was a job that I could not have done by myself."

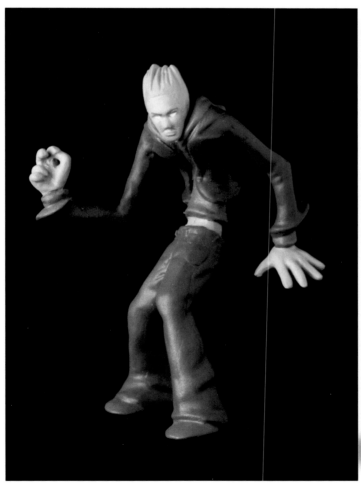

SEGURA INC.

LOCATION: Chicago, USA

PROFILE: Carlos Segura was born in Santiago, Cuba and moved to the United States in 1965 at the age of nine. He is completely self-taught as a designer, he started with promotional material for his own band as a teenager, then got a job as a production artist and went on to work for various ad agencies (Marsteller, Foote Cone and Belding, Young and Rubicam, Ketchum, DDB Needham, BBDO, etc.). Finding that he was not happy creatively, he quit to found Segura Inc. in 1991. The firm is multi-faceted and has various branches: Segura Inc. covers design, advertising, branding, corporate identity and print collateral; Segura Interactive is the web and new media division of Segura Inc.; [T-26], the digital type foundry, focuses on the creation, distribution and sale of original typefaces; Thickface is an independent record label and 5inch is an online outlet for pre-designed CDRs.

MISSION: Despite its wide range of activities, Segura Inc. is a company of only eight full-time members: "We blend as much 'fine art' into 'commercial art' as possible, while believing that 'communication that doesn't take a chance, doesn't stand a chance'. Graphic design, print advertising, logos, catalogues, annual reports, brochures, corporate identities, posters and new media are not the only things we do, but they are some of the things we do best. Whatever the medium, we create marketing messages that people notice and respond to with a distinct sense of style and simplicity that stands the test of time."

CLIENTS: Corbis, The Alternative Pick, Q101 Radio, Swatch, The Wall Street Journal, T26 Type Foundry, 5inch.com

DANGEROUSLY BOLD

CLIENT: Express Jeans, USA

BRIEF: "As part of an ongoing campaign by Express Jeans, Express commissioned designers from all over the world to develop their jeans tags."

CONCEPT: "To create tags for the jeans as useful objects, (this was our own concept). We were given permission to do whatever we wanted, so long as we used the phrase 'dangerously bold'."

SOLUTION: The three solutions we came up with were; the silk-screen and stitched ipod/phone/camera case; the template and the wallet tags, all of which act as the jeans tag, but can then be removed and have their own individual uses."

LESSON: "That taking a chance can pay off. We were the only firm to present (and sell) tags as objects (as opposed to standard printed ones that are simply removed and discarded). The tags remain in the hands of the customer as useful items long after the purchase; keeping the brand in their lives."

There are a thousand ways to attract attention, but once you've got the potential client-to-be looking in your direction how do you ensure that they take the next step? From an established creative company of hardened professionals to a footloose young freelancer, the issues are still the same: a designer with their own particular brand of work needs to come together with a client who is looking for something that they particularly need. A rapport needs to be established and the better they understand one another, the better the chances are that the result will please all concerned.

What are your tactics for first meetings with clients?

JORK ANDRE DIETER: "When you are going to meet clients, of course it is important to have had a shave and look clean and cared for – I do that anyway. But what you wear is not so relevant. I pay a lot of attention to punctuality and good preparation, like being well informed beforehand about who the clients are and what they do. Everything else is a case of them having to take me as they find me. The main thing is to give the impression that I'm capable of providing the service that they require. I am a service provider in this instance."

FRANÇOIS CHALET: "I try and charm them. I also try and make clear who I am and what I want to and can contribute. I don't always have to be the right one for the job but if I really want to have it then I try and charm even more – sometimes it works."

SIMON DIXON, DIXONBAXI: "To be ourselves and try to explain who we are and what we do in as relaxed and simple a way as possible. We usually know a little about their company but will research a bit more if we don't understand what they do. Other than that it is a matter of fitting together and building a rhythm. We have a particular set of comments, anecdotes and projects that we talk about but leave room to discuss a prospective client's own thoughts, or react to a discussion. We try to avoid complete monologues as it gets dull for both parties. A conversation has always been a stronger way to connect with people. Often if you deliver a monologue it is great at the time but the memory fades after the event. We have more positive responses when we chat rather than try to deliver a monologue. The opposite is true for creative presentations though. For those we prepare and deliver a little more theatre, directing the proceedings to a climax."

What do you wear for your first meeting? Is it suits or sneakers, surnames or first names? Do you dress and behave like a "creative" – you are after all part of the entertainment – or do you smarten up and act sensible?

FANNY KHOO, FLINK: "I'm afraid I haven't got any suits and pretty much dress the way I'm comfortable with. That has never been a problem with clients."

SIMON DIXON, DIXONBAXI: "Depends on the client. We don't 'dress up' specifically but do try to feel relaxed. Clothes that suit us are more important. Ultimately it is about your personality and how you deliver your ideas. We are not entertainers but do need to connect with people, so a little charm, intelligence and energy helps the process. Relaxed. positive and interested are better than any suit or smart Prada top. It's like flirting or meeting someone for the first time. Cheap after-shave doesn't cut the mustard but a bit of confidence and chat will. As to acting like a creative I'm not sure what that entails. The type of clients we work with are regular, smart and successful people. They meet many types of skilled and talented people so a specific creative approach would be redundant. It would actually hamper the process, as you, look contrived or false. We act the same way we would in every meeting. That way there is no let down later – we are what we are and if that's OK then we'll work well for people."

FRANÇOIS CHALET: "I have a Diesel deodorant stick and usually an amusing T-shirt and I arrive with my laptop. Oh what am I talking about, it's ages since I had a first meeting with a client for a pitch. The last time was with Dentsu in Tokyo and I bought a Helmut Lang shirt for the occasion. Mostly people contact me by email or telephone and we meet each other at a later date – or my agent meets them."

"When in Rome..." Are customs in different countries really that different? Do you have to dress smarter in London or present differently in China?

SIMON DIXON, DIXONBAXI: "No. You're being hired for your work. We try to understand the client's world and how we would work within it but we are UK-based and therefore will bring a UK personality to our appearance. The work hopefully functions in any language. A little learning, good briefing and applied intelligence should lead to work that has relevance to other cultures."

JONATHAN BARNBROOK: "The social thing is a bit harder but design is universal and good ideas are universal long as you are not making some kind of really bad social faux pas with the visual language you are using, then people understand the thought processes beyond language."

FANNY KHOO, FLINK: "I would say that there's a huge cultural difference in the way we address clients or just people. Say, between Singapore and Belgium for example, Belgians are usually a lot more subtle and one has to learn to listen hard and read between the lines! Singaporeans are more open in that particular sense."

Do you wait until the client calls you and asks you to pitch?

FRANÇOIS CHALET: "That's how it has been so far and I think that's how it is best. I have always had bad experiences when I was re-commended but the client didn't already know my work. I think a good approach is to make sure that as many people as possible see your work and hope that some of them become interested in it and then contact you."

SIMON DIXON, DIXONBAXI: "We contact prospects if we hear about a lead or project. Otherwise we react to calls, meetings or referrals. We rarely pitch and never without a fee. If we are called for a pitch we would usually ask to meet them to do a credential meeting before agreeing to pitch. And even then we often won't pitch as it is counter to how we produce work or develop a genuine relationship with a client."

FANNY KHOO, FLINK: "Last year, we did a fair amount of pitching, which hasn't really paid off in terms of costs. It does allow us to expand our portfolio and skills though. Mostly, potential clients call with a specific brief and invite us to pitch."

Is it worth sending in a portfolio to desired clients on the off chance that they might call you in for a meeting?

SIMON DIXON, DIXONBAXI: "We have sent videotapes and booklets to prospective clients. It is really a numbers game; you need to send a certain amount to get a hit. It is a tool we revert to only on a few occasions. We develop projects and relationships over time and hope-fully continue to work with people once we are onboard. The largest part of our work comes from referral by existing clients or contacts to prospective clients. If we do well people talk about it and it leads to more work."

FRANÇOIS CHALET: "If I want to work for someone, then I make it clear to them and send them my portfolio. Whether he or she then calls me is another matter."

Is your portfolio virtual or hard copy – online or on paper?

SIMON DIXON, DIXONBAXI: "Both. It depends on circumstance. In many instances we talk about us, our way of working and the results. Often we show very little work. If we do, a videotape, a digital presentation and a small 'leave behind' booklet suffice."

FANNY KHOO, FLINK: "It's mostly online but we have a printed version of our portfolio as well, and we've also developed a couple of case studies on PDF."

FRANÇOIS CHALET: "I have my own homepage and an agent in Paris who has me on his homepage. I also have a book about my work that is an invaluable portfolio."

When submitting a design, do you give the client alternative options or not?

SIMON DIXON, DIXONBAXI: "It all depends on the project, client and expectancy. We prefer one clear route."

JONATHAN BARNBROOK: "We give Powerbook presentations. Usually we offer three or four alternatives to the client and because it is a process of refinement, you start off with a few ideas and work down to one that everybody is happy with."

FRANÇOIS CHALET: "I nearly always give three options, I think that's a good way to let the client feel that they have a choice. I believe that good solutions come when there is a dialogue."

KASIA KORCZAK: "You should always propose to a client more than you think they will accept, because it is much easier to strip down an idea than to regret not having pushed it in the direction you wanted to go."

What are the advantages or disadvantages of having an agency or contract company between you and the client? Are some clients so alien that you need an interpreter to deal with them?

SIMON DIXON, DIXONBAXI: "If they are too alien then we're not the right fit for them. We usually find that after meeting and chatting we either gel with a prospective client or don't. If we do we work with them, if not we don't. The idea of using a third party is counter to how we work. It muddies the water and basically masks deficiencies in a relationship."

FRANÇOIS CHALET: "My agent in Paris func-tions like a cushion. They also have the right degree of distance from my work and can therefore ask the clients for more money. If it wasn't for them, some clients, like Mitsubishi, would certainly never have come to me."

JONATHAN BARNBROOK: "Having an agency between you and the client tends to make things much more complicated because the agency are often more interested in keeping the account, for example, and they might have a tendency to take fewer chances. I think it is one of the worst things when other people present your work."

ANDY MUELLER

LOCATION: Los Angeles, USA

PROFILE: Andy Mueller is a full time Art Director for Lakai Limited Footwear and Girl Skateboards. The art department at Girl is known as the Art Dump and has five other members. Mueller studied Communications and Media Studies at the University of Illinois, which involved a combination of media history, media ethics and photojournalism. "As far as graphic design goes, I have yet to take a class", he says, "I'm self taught; It's just been a lot of experimenting, learning through trial and error and sitting in front of various Apple Computer products for the last ten years or so."

MISSION: "I work with a simple, honest and fun approach and try not to tie myself down to just one definitive style. I like to experiment with ideas and processes and try to make my work progress. I mostly do photography and graphic design. My main focus so far has been on music packaging design, skateboard and snowboard design, posters of all sorts and graphics for T-shirts and accessories, as well as my own personal artwork."

CLIENTS: Girl Skateboards, Lakai Limited Footwear, Fourstar Clothing, Ruby Republic Clothing, Chocolate Skateboards, Clae Footwear, The Quiet Life, Burton Snowboards, XXX Snowboards, Jade Tree Records, Thrill Jockey Records, Electra Records, Capitol Records, Anthem, Bail etc.

LAKAI POSTERS

CLIENT: Lakai Limited Footwear and Girl Skateboards, Los Angeles, USA

BRIEF: "I work in-house for Lakai Limited Footwear, so in some ways I'm partially the client. I enjoy this as it gives me a lot of creative freedom!"

CONCEPT: "To create visually appealing imagery to promote skateboard tours, events and demos."

SOLUTION: "I am always drawing and doodling in my sketch books as well as collecting ideas from the outside world. I try to have a supply of images and ideas ready to go for any project that I might be working on."

LESSON: "Every time I work on a poster (or design), I continue to learn that it's best to keep it simple and to try not to over design it."

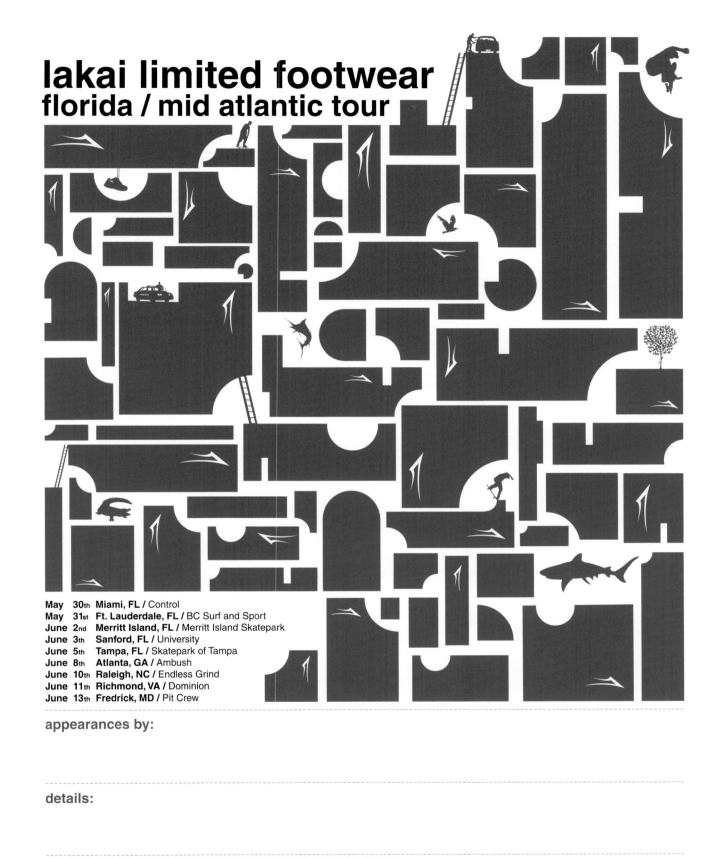

lakai limited footwear
florida / mid atlantic tour

May   30th **Miami, FL /** Control
May   31st **Ft. Lauderdale, FL /** BC Surf and Sport
June 2nd **Merritt Island, FL /** Merritt Island Skatepark
June 3th **Sanford, FL /** University
June 5th **Tampa, FL /** Skatepark of Tampa
June 8th **Atlanta, GA /** Ambush
June 10th **Raleigh, NC /** Endless Grind
June 11th **Richmond, VA /** Dominion
June 13th **Fredrick, MD /** Pit Crew

appearances by:

details:

lakai CRAILTAP.COM

SEB JARNOT

LOCATION: Nîmes, France

PROFILE: "I studied at BRASSART, a graphic art school in Tours, France and graduated in 1992. I learned a huge amount after I decided to become a freelance illustrator in 1997 – I did a lot of work over two years but with practically no commissions. I didn't do any internships, but after college worked as a graphic designer in a small agency in Nîmes for three years."

MISSION: "I am an image-maker, I don't feel like an illustrator. People say that my line is full of energy and tension. I experiment with drawings without being limited by styles. I often do figurative things but I'm also very interested in abstraction, minimalism and accidents. The large range of styles I use is both a strength and a weakness because it means that it is sometimes difficult for others to recognise and understand my work."

CLIENTS: F Communications (an electronic music label based in Paris), Wieden and Kennedy, Amsterdam; Libération, Paris; and many French magazines.

JAMESON

CLIENT: Fame Advertising, Ogilvy and Mather, Sydney, Australia

BRIEF: "The goal was to target young people at parties with something strange and fun, for a new drink based on Irish whisky and lemon, created by Jameson."

CONCEPT: "It was quite simple really. The Art Director liked my sketchy style so he sent me some layouts he had made based on a few drawings that he had downloaded from my website. He asked me to make some compositions with the bottle and the tag-line 'green and twisted'."

SOLUTION: "I wanted to make weird images that question people. Something that was easy, fun and complex. For me the particular challenge was to make visuals that could be strong enough by only using lines."

LESSON: "It is difficult to tell you what I learnt from this project, I only made two drawings and then the project stopped. I think you learn a lot when you have the vision of the project in progress and later a vision in the street. The second vision is missing. It was apparently rejected because the client wanted photographs rather than illustrations. The Art Director asked me for something radical and I had fun doing it, but I think there was little chance of it ever being accepted."

NIKE

CLIENT: Wieden and Kennedy, Amsterdam, The Netherlands. Art Director, Merete Busk

BRIEF: Produce illustrations for Nike apparel advertising campaign.

CONCEPT: "The clients had a record sleeve that I did for St. Germain (F Communications) and were interested in the movement and energy that emanated from this drawing. They wanted this feeling for their campaign. The project was graphically very ambitious and it was my first international print campaign. I didn't just want to express physical energy with the images, I wanted to bring in the idea of mental shots through the abstraction."

SOLUTION: "They didn't like the first series of sketches that I did, but after that I talked to them and understood that they were open-minded towards abstraction, which led to a result that was really free and obvious; based on sensations."

LESSON: "I learned that this kind of project can take you into areas where you couldn't go by yourself. For me it was a huge experience that allowed me to mix both graphic research and large-scale public exposure."

VASAVA
ARTWORKS

LOCATION: Barcelona, Spain

PROFILE: Vasava is a communications studio founded in Barcelona in 1997. It comprises a team of ten people from various disciplines. Specialist areas include: corporate identity, magazine design, books, print, exhibitions, typography, websites and interactive projects.

MISSION: "Any medium can be an inspiration for another, that's the good thing about the connected world. It is increasingly easy to create parallels because trends are incorporating ever more disciplines and it is easy to initiate an exchange of ideas. In reality everything influences you, moulds you and changes your perception of things. The hardest thing of all then is to create your own language — unique and genuine, without obvious influences."

CLIENTS: Campari, Camper, Canal Satélite Digital, Caroche Jeans, Centre de Cultura Contemprànea de Barcelona, Cosmos Records, Fundació Joan Miró, Le Cool, Midday, Pantone, Real Club Deportivo Español, Royal Paper, Starfish, Silvia Prada, the British Council, Volkswagen, etc.

ANDRES GARCIA

CLIENT: Andres Garcia, Valencia, Spain

BRIEF: "The objective was to create a brand identity for this fashion label's spring/summer collection 2004. They wanted a fresh and spontaneous image."

CONCEPT: "We wanted to communicate that the Andres Garcia brand had evolved and had changed how they present themselves. Everything should change but not too radically. We wanted to do a simple studio session, with small complementary objects, initials of the brand's name and some graphic resources interacting with the image."

SOLUTION: "First of all we produced hours and hours worth of small drawings of things starting with the same initials, as idea sources, then we used two models and sixteen pictures to present the new philosophy. The photographer Leila Méndez helped define the styling."

LESSON: "Every single project is different."

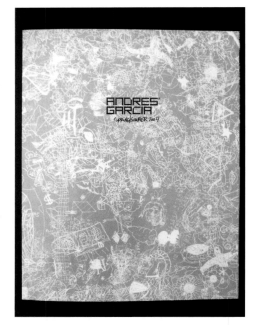

Photo: Leila Méndez

ENAMEL

LOCATION: Tokyo, Japan

PROFILE: Enamels's two partners started working together in 2001. Beforehand, Ryoji Ishioka graduated in Textile Design from Tama Art University and Sayuri Ishioka graduated in Display Design from Musashino Art University. Their bag designing was, however, self-taught. Ishioka took an internship at a graphic design company for three years while he was still at college, and worked as a designer for two-and-a-half years after graduating. He found the experience invaluable because: "I was able to see the whole process of design work. It was also good to experience physical limitation, not everyone can experience working three days straight without taking sleep". After graduating from college, Ishioka worked as a contract designer at a clothing company. Here, she says, she rapidly discovered that working as a corporate designer was not her style.

MISSION: "We design like designers. We are about ideas and strong visuals and striving not to be in poor taste."

CLIENTS: Outlets include: FACTORY, Tokyo; Points de Suspension, Tokyo; W-VISION, Kumamoto, Plaguesearch, Hiroshima; Maxalot, Barcelona, Spain.

BAGS

CLIENT: Self-initiated bag and graphic design project.

BRIEF: "The clients in this case are the customers who buy our products and our bags. We try to deal with stores and customers directly for each of the pieces as much as possible because we want to get to know the people behind the faces who sell our bags and who use our products. Their needs can be considered to be our brief."

CONCEPT: Each season, Enamel come up with a new bag and accessories collection: The first collection was about stripes, the second used reversed jeans pockets and printed images for a "sloppy look". For the third collection the idea for the handle came from the rope from an S&M game with six different types of religious-style visuals and hand-colouring with coloured pencils. The fourth season's bags had porcelain handles like tea-cups.

SOLUTION: Enamel hire people to help make their bags and do all their own printing. For the fourth collection, they also created an exhibition for the products.

LESSON: "It was a challenge for us to think about the relationship between space, products and installation."

enamel. 4th.

enamel.4
Child's puzzle, 2003
Happy Birthday, Benio.

DESPERADO

CLIENT: LOOK INC., Tokyo, Japan

BRIEF: "Each year the Desperado clothing shop in Tokyo invites artists and designers to do exhibitions by using in-store window displays. The public can buy these exhibits. We were asked to design the flyer for the nine participating artists and designers."

CONCEPT: The idea came while the designers were throwing away junk mail from their own letterbox. "Desperado is basically a girls' fashion store. The client wanted to differentiate it from other similar shops, so the interior designer, Ima, came up with the idea of using the shop's window display to create a 'shop in shop in Desperado'."

SOLUTION: "Although people in Tokyo are not used to buying art products like they buy clothes, the client decided to try selling the goods displayed in the exhibition. We were asked to announce this fascinating event on a flyer. We used postcard-sized direct-mail advertising for flyers and to announce each exhibition. We had to send out a total of nine different flyers throughout the year. But we wanted to avoid people getting tired of receiving junk flyers, so we had to come up with different ideas each time."

LESSON: "There is a gap between the people who come to see the exhibition and the people who come to buy clothes, and I would somehow like to reduce this gap."

KLAUS HAAPANIEMI

LOCATION: Italy, UK, Finland

PROFILE: Haapaniemi is a Finnish-born free-lance illustrator and designer who creates concepts and comes up with key graphics for fashion companies. He is someone who generally prefers his work to speak for itself, rather than waste too many words on it, and his only elucidation to his modus operandi is: "Sometimes I work with a team and sometimes without, it depends on the project".

MISSION: "I learned everything that I know before I was five years old. Since them every thing has been pretty much the same but with minor adjustments in content."

CLIENTS: Bantam, Diesel, OMAG-solutions, etc.

BANTAM

CLIENT: Bantam, Milan, Italy

BRIEF: "To do fashion prints and illustrations and all the promotional material for the new collection."

CONCEPT: "New Baroque from the Italian east-coast meets Pax Romana, aka: 'how to punish the barbarian hordes'. When Germanicus, with his legions, liberated lands that are now part of Germany from ravaging barbarian tribes, he had a dream of uniting all the peoples and bringing peace to the living; to build cities on the empty frontier; teach their children how to read and write and create a real society in the middle of nowhere. It is not yet working completely, but now we all want to live in peace and harmony and we've got all the things that peace can bring us, like welfare and quality of life. Yet still we want to conquer others and take their property or lands. But as one great man said, 'war is not the answer', so the best way to conquer the barbarians is not just by killing them all. The way to enslave their minds is through their hearts and souls." This theme, says Haapaniemi, was inspired by watching Mel Gibson's "Passion of Christ".

SOLUTION: "In true Italian-fashion style, we printed a catalogue that told the story of how to conquer without bloodshed and then we distributed this publication worldwide. The collection theme was basically working with the same elements but it was bit more feminine."

LESSON: "It re-enforced our experience that even if a budget is non-existent, our imagination is never-ending."

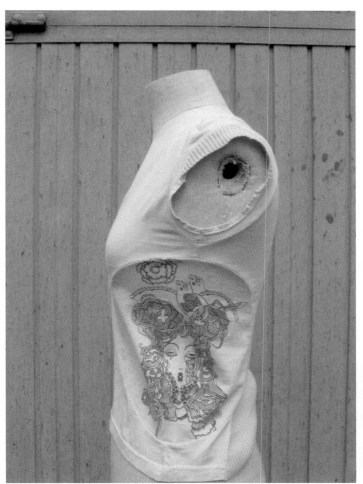

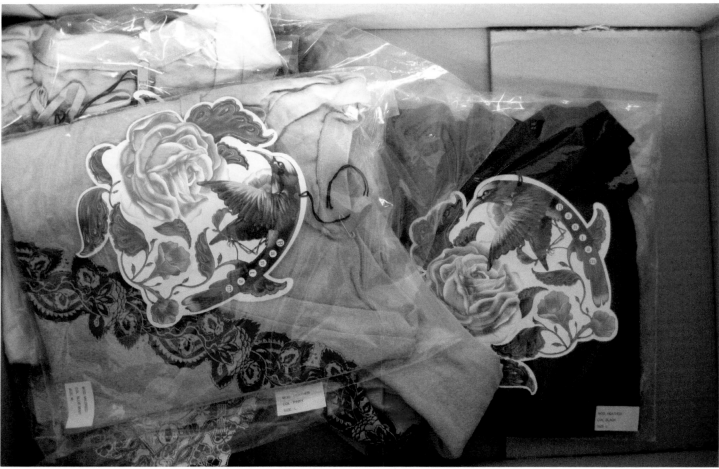

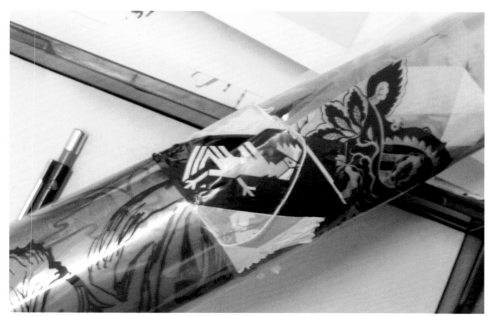

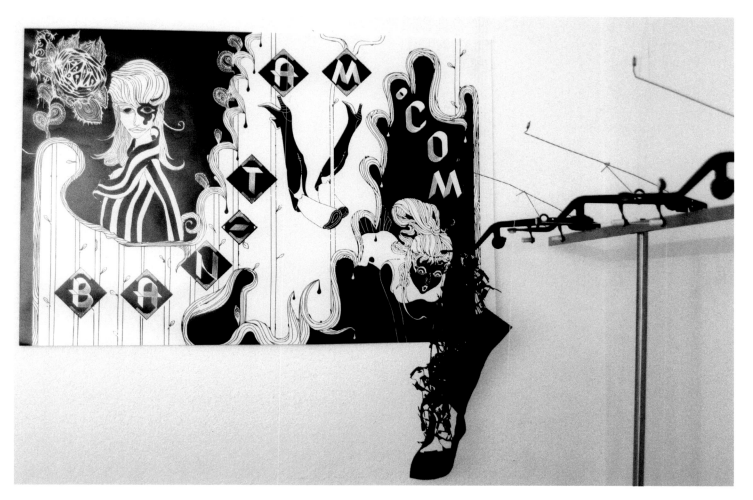

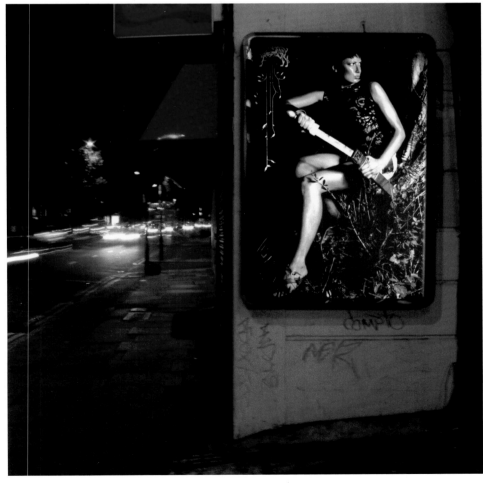

Whether they like it or not, if they need to earn a living, no designer is exempt from the tasks of finding clients, acquiring work and establishing a reputation in the marketplace. The techniques involved are anathema to some and an enjoyable game to others. Strategies vary, but the main rule seems to be to make sure you hang on to your integrity during the course of the ride.

What is the value of contact with other design companies?
MARTIN WOODTLI: "What do you mean by 'value'? I have no desire to toady around in the hope of getting business contacts. I don't think that this works in the long run either. I find individual commitment important for other designers as well as oneself and the contact can be exciting because it is about friendly exchange."
FULGURO: "It's always good, but not very frequent; the impact of networking on our activities is very slow. You wait for years before a contact appears to be effective."
FLORIAN PFEFFER, JUNG + PFEFFER: "Exchange, friction, arguments, fun, confusion, doubts, love …but that counts for all human contacts, be it designers, clients or other beings."
FANNY KHOO, FLINK: "[The value for me is] massive creative input, since Flink is much too small and we don't have enough like-minded individuals around. I really like being part of the big picture, so networking within the creative field is really important to me."

Is it worth going to "Designer Friday"-style gatherings, trade fairs, symposia and conferences? Why? Are they just for corporate nerds on expense accounts or is there something to be gained from mingling and exchanging ideas with the competition?
MARTIN WOODTLI: "International exchange can be fascinating because it can turn out that you have more in common with designers from Asia, for example, than with your neighbour in your own country with whom you may share a cultural background but be mentally from another planet."
FULGURO: "It's interesting to see what is being done, what kind of design is being produced, what is new, or to show our work and to make contacts, but it's not easy. We also try to go to other gatherings, like art exhibitions, architecture events, concerts or bars to see something other than design for a change."

What about having agents and websites where you can display your work? Do you use such services or have you done so in the past and of what benefit were / are they?
MARTIN WOODTLI: "I have my own website but not to promote my own work — none of it is displayed there. It functions purely as a contact address."
FULGURO: "A website is cheaper; we have two. It's a good way to show some stuff and to control what and how we want to communicate. But the effect is hard to quantify. We don't really know if our websites have an impact or not. We are just starting out with our professional activities and haven't had time to look for places to show our work."
FANNY KHOO, FLINK: "Flink has been linked from other portal sites though, which has helped a lot in terms of establishing a reputation."
DIPESH PANDYA: "I have had a selection of my work on an agent's website in the past. Unfortunately I don't know if it generated any interest, since the Parisian agent in question never managed to find me one single job in the two years that I was 'represented' by them. I am in the process of preparing my own website."

Is the "old boy network" still functioning? How big a role does knowing, being related to or having been to college with someone in the potential client's office play in tipping the scales in your favour?

MARTIN WOODTLI: "It is easy to get recognition in your own circle of people with the same interests. It is more challenging to try to place your own interests in new and unfamiliar surroundings without simply selling yourself, but perhaps to push something new for yourself and the environment instead."

FULGURO: "We hope it is still functioning, but not too much...We'll find out when our old mates are older and have jobs in high positions where they make the decisions and can give us some jobs!"

DIPESH PANDYA: "Yes I think it is still functioning for the same stupid reasons that it always has – people being blinded by name-dropping."

FLORIAN PFEFFER, JUNG + PFEFFER: "The problem for the client is that he takes a risk when hiring a designer. He is 'buying the cat in the sack' (a German saying which means you have to buy the cat without knowing what it looks like). So anything that enhances the client's belief in a successful outcome will work in your favour. Personal contact can be one of those trust factors; others are, reputation, recommendation, company size, client lists, successful collaborations in the past etc. There is nothing wrong with any of them."

FANNY KHOO, FLINK: "Often, knowing someone from somewhere makes it easier to get around. That rule applies practically everywhere. However, it is your own merit that will make the difference in the end."

Social networking: is being a party animal and being seen in all the right places a more acceptable form of networking?

MARTIN WOODTLI: "I go to parties to have fun, not to look for work. I don't find having a healthy presence and self-confidence in one's commitment reprehensible. Whether this takes place in the Champagne Bar or on the Web is a matter of personal preference; one is more analogue, the other more digital."

FULGURO: "It is not our style. We don't show off much. Our director at college (écal) used to tell us to go to such events 'to see and to be seen'. Since it worked well for him, we guess it should work for everybody."

DIPESH PANDYA: "I don't know whether it is more acceptable, but it can definitely be fun."

FLORIAN PFEFFER, JUNG + PFEFFER: "Having a drink together can also be one of those trust factors, but try not to get completely drunk or you will end up either making a monkey out of yourself or your potential client."

Does it pay to schmooze?

CARTLIDGE LEVENE: "To survive in any industry you must be known. You can have the best product in the world but if no one knows about it, you won't go far. Any form of networking is healthy for a design studio. Resonating within a design 'community' is a good thing. Being known by your clients is a good thing. Displaying your work online, in magazines or in books is a good thing. Socialising and exchanging ideas with other designers is a good thing. Engaging in all of these not only makes you a known 'player' in the industry, but also continually exposes you to new ideas and potential opportunities."

FLORIAN PFEFFER, JUNG + PFEFFER: "It pays to be honest. If you schmooze honestly, that's fine by me."

DIPESH PANDYA: "From experience, yes. Everybody likes to schmooze now and again."

FULGURO: "If 'schmooze' means what we think it means (lécher le cul), we definitely think that it can pay off in the short term, but after a while people who get 'schmoozed' also get bored of being 'schmoozed' by the same people. So they change 'schmoozers'. Moral: don't 'schmooze'."

MARTIN WOODTLI: "Is it worth playing this game? To have commitment and not simply suck up to supply a service; to question the norm and try to be above the average; to have your own obsessions and eclectic creations instead of this post-modern icon stealing; that is worth it!"

RINZEN

LOCATION: Brisbane, Australia

PROFILE: Rinzen is a "collaborative" of five individuals: Steve Alexander, Rilla Alexander, Adrian Clifford, Craig Redman and Karl Maier who all studied Graphic Design at the Queensland College of Art, Australia. Rinzen works on a range of client and personal projects — in print and web design, illustration, font design, characters, animation and music. Founded in 2000, the company has a "flat business structure where majority votes decide all crucial decisions". The collaborators are all designers. "Rinzen is the intersecting point of our common interests, visions, and abilities — this was the inspiration for our initial grouping." All the team had previous working experience. "From a purely business perspective it is essential to have worked in the design industry prior to beginning your own business. It also allows you to develop creatively and determine your own direction, and gives you the impetus to change the way you set up your own organisation. We knew we wanted to be flexible, to enjoy our work and to make time for our own projects — we learnt how to do this by learning what not to do beforehand. Our previous employers ranged from a small socially-aware design group to firms specialising in Corporate Identity. Steve and I Rilla also worked in London, Berlin and Zurich during the dot.com boom, designing the Wallpaper* Website for a large German new-media firm."

MISSION: "The group is active in self-initiated and contributor-based projects, participating in numerous online and print-based graphic works, as well as directing the RMX [graphic remixes] series of projects.'Play' is a key role in the creative process, and is not limited to 'free art' projects; any and all visual solutions are solved through developing and applying the results of creative 'play'. We embrace collaboration as a valuable and gloriously unpredictable learning opportunity."

CLIENTS: Diesel, Mooks, Vogue, Nylon, Absolute Vodka, Warner, as well as agencies such as TBWA, Wieden and Kennedy and Wink.

UNDER BIFROST

CLIENT: Queensland Art Gallery, Brisbane, Australia

BRIEF: "The mural design for the Queensland Art Gallery arose as a collaborative project put forward by the gallery who suggested we work with Prins, an artist from Sydney. The creative brief was left entirely to us."

CONCEPT: "The piece is about cycles. The title 'Under Bifrost' refers to the Norse rainbow bridge linking the mortal world to the world of the gods; you can see this bridge represented over the castle in the centre of the design. From this central element, the picture is built around cycles through contrasting poles; the cycle of death and rebirth, mortality and immortality. This is reinforced through the colour and toning that runs from dark to light, and also narratively in the fox and rabbit chase in the foreground."

SOLUTION: "The final painted mural was seven metres long and four metres high, with the wooden sculpture by Prins hung in a central position, about a metre away from the wall itself."

LESSON: "Apart from extending the Rinzen oeuvre through the thematic basis of the piece, we also had the chance to hear and see reactions from the viewing public as we were painting the piece. Over the course of a week, visitors to the gallery would pass by and comment, or give their idea of what the design was about, which was in turn interesting, amusing, baffling and enlightening. The immediacy of the feedback was a big change from the normal deployment of our designs, which when printed usually go off into the world on their own."

ZERO GATE

CLIENT: Zero Gate department store, Tokyo, Japan.

BRIEF: "Design a Christmas shop display for the exterior of the four-storey Zero Gate department store. The piece should be approached as though it was a hip-hop music video for a song called 'Christmas wrap' featuring MC Santa Claus. The approved direction also requested that the illustration incorporate frames of action or a sense of movement."

CONCEPT: "The major goal was to produce a great outcome within the confines of the supplied concept. It can be quite difficult to work within a very specific brief as it allows little room for creative interpretation."

SOLUTION: "We worked within the specifications to illustrate the idea in an entertaining way. We tied the design together through a stack of speakers in the shape of a Christmas tree. The illustrations were realised as a large-scale diorama in Japan and also used on Christmas cards."

LESSON: "Working with and beyond an established concept."

VALLEY

CLIENT: City of Brisbane, Queensland, Australia

BRIEF: "Create a promotional campaign for 'The Valley', the city's shopping, entertainment and restaurant districts that incorporates Chinatown. The key imagery should not contain people or scenes of shopping, dancing or eating."

CONCEPT: "While the brief for the actual subject matter was very open, we felt that the illustrations should give a sense of place and show the 'real' Valley atmosphere."

SOLUTION: The first picture reflects the history of the area from the first European settlers who arrived from London in 1848. The second, the boom years of the 1950s, and a third image recognises of the area's cultural diversity, featuring the lion at the gates of Chinatown.

LESSON: "Further confirming the importance of keeping our work 'collectable', be it for a promotional campaign or as 'art'."

CARTLIDGE
LEVENE

LOCATION: London, UK

PROFILE: Ian Cartildge and Adam Levene worked at Conran Design and Michael Peters respectively before meeting at the Design Solution. They founded Cartlidge Levene in 1987 having worked together for two years. Hector Pottie, Melissa Price and Simon Anderson joined the company in early 2001. Hector previously worked at Blue Source and also worked with Melissa in the 1990s at Metadesign London. Before that Melissa worked at Imagination. Simon joined the company straight from college.

MISSION: "Our approach is simple; we are passionate about design and communication and are driven by excellence. Our core attributes are listening, solving, creating and delivering. We are a tight-knit team of five and form close working relationships with our clients. With seventeen years of experience, we have a proven track record of delivering the highest standards of design. We are inspired by meeting a challenge and solving problems. We believe in graphic communication and the value it brings."

CLIENTS: Architects' Registration Board, Architecture Foundation, Barbican Arts Centre, Carlisle Group, Crafts Council, Compass Group PLC, Derwent Valley, Design Council, Design Museum, Dexia Group, Eye Magazine, FSB/Allgood, Future Systems, Glasgow 1999, Hewlett-Packard Laboratories, Housing Design Awards, Magnum Photos, Marylebone Cricket Club, Millennium Lofts, Millennium Point, NatWest, Office of the Deputy Prime Minister, Patel Taylor, RIBA, Selfridges and Co., Sergison Bates, Shell, Society of Typographic Designers, Tate Modern.

SOLID AIR

CLIENT: Crafts Council, London, UK

BRIEF: Create a marketing campaign, including posters, leaflets, catalogue, launch invite and exhibition graphics for an exhibition of four artists working in glass, at the Crafts Council.

CONCEPT: "As the show contained the work of four artists, no single item of work could be used as a 'hero' image. Our challenge was to create an image that formed the identity of the show and would work across all material."

SOLUTION: "The prism graphic was created as a simple visual metaphor representing glass, light, colour, reflection, refraction and the fact that the show featured the work of four artists. The prism graphic had to be flexible and was used in various ways across all material from a single mark to linear texture and pattern. We came up with the prism graphic relatively quickly but continued to explore other possible solutions. Various routes were developed and discussed with the client but everyone kept coming back to the prism for its simplicity and visual strength."

LESSON: "Simple and beautiful is always best. The most important achievement is persuading the client and all involved to believe this. Often, the purity of a graphic or idea can become watered down by adding too much 'noise' to it. The art of restraint in a graphic design studio is a valuable thing."

Solid Air
New work in glass

11 April—
16 June 2002

Free entry

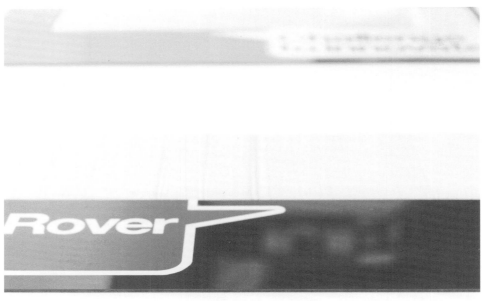

FUTURE TALK CAFÉ

CLIENT: Design Council, London, UK

BRIEF: Create an exhibition space for the Design Council at the British Chamber of Commerce annual conference.

CONCEPT: "The Future Talk Café was designed to be an area of calm within the bustling exhibition hall. We produced the exhibition in collaboration with the architect Cherie Yeo."

SOLUTION: "We created an exhibition space and relaxing environments where delegates could take a break from the conference hall, have a coffee and learn about e-commerce."

NO PICNIC

CLIENT: Crafts Council, London, UK

BRIEF: Design an exhibition for the Crafts Council focusing on attitudes towards products and production among contemporary designers and makers.

CONCEPT: "A key element for this show was the interaction with visitors."

SOLUTION: "We developed a graphic identity through the design of a sticker system which became a simple mechanism for exhibit labelling, as well as allowing visitors to record their comments by sticking them on the wall space provided. We produced the exhibition in collaboration with Adjaye Russel architects."

CONTEMPORARY JAPANESE JEWELLERY

CLIENT: Crafts Council, London, UK

BRIEF: Design the marketing identity, exhibition graphics and gallery guide for the Craft Council's touring exhibition.

CONCEPT: "Working closely with Stickland Coombe architects, we produced a labelling system for the display cases that played on the sushi-style conveyor belt concept."

SOLUTION: "This worked in conjunction with our design for the printed gallery guide."

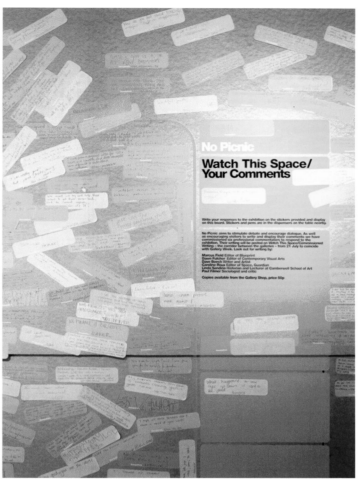

No Picnic

Watch This Space/
Your Comments

Write your responses to the exhibition on the stickers provided and display on this board. Stickers and pens are in the dispensers on the table nearby.

No Picnic aims to stimulate debate and encourage dialogue. As well as encouraging visitors to write and display their comments we have commissioned six professional commentators to respond to the exhibition. Their writing will be posted on Watch This Space/Commissioned Writing — the corridor between the galleries — from 21 July to coincide with Gallery Week. Look out for writing by:

Marcus Field Editor of Blueprint
Dawn Fulcher Editor of Contemporary Visual Arts
Dave Beech Writer and Artist
Caroline Roux Editor of Space, Guardian
Linda Sandino Historian and Lecturer at Camberwell School of Art
Paul Filmer Sociologist and critic

Copies available from the Gallery Shop, price 50p

KENZO MINAMI

LOCATION: New York, USA

PROFILE: "I studied Western Philosophy for a year in Japan and then took a BFA in Industrial Design at Parsons School of Design. I started working as a set designer for film and TV while still at school. I was also doing various projects with the M.I.T. Media Lab team as an interface designer, so I guess they were like internships for me, though I've never really done anything as an 'intern'. I eventually started shooting my own short films, doing motion graphics, and 3D animation and became partner/director/art director of a company called Panoptic Inc. – which essentially became my 'day job'. My own art work and paintings are completely separate and started as a reaction to all the commercial work I'd done."

MISSION: "I am interested in mixing diverse ideas and styles to create a whole new self-contained meaning, system, nuance, idea, or aesthetic; like Eric Satie meets Megadeth and Eco meets Douglas Adams – controlled chaos. There are sets of logic, systems, and rules of my own that make sense to myself, so despite the apparent chaotic nature that my pieces sometimes have there is some sort of order and unity, both logically and visually – at least to me there is. Sometimes when I take styles and contexts and swap them, something else interesting happens as well. If you have skill and good taste, you can manage to make it work in a neat way. But there is sometimes a gap, where it seems almost forced together. I am very fascinated by this 'gap', it has a curious effect and creates a completely new feeling."

CLIENTS: Nike, Raf Simons, Colette, International DeeJay Gigolo, VH1, Seven New York, I Heart, Adidas, Mogul Electro, Studio Distribution, Tribeca Grand Hotel, Flaunt Magazine, Blackbook, XLR8R, Lodown, i-D, W, Addict, WAD, Mined, Pour le Victoire, Heavy Change, and Flip the Script by Surface 2 Air.

RAF SIMONS

CLIENT: Raf Simons, Paris, France

BRIEF: This was really two projects: The first was to design an invitation for Raf Simons' first fashion show outside Europe, in NYC. The other was to draw a portrait of the fashion designer for an article in Colette magazine. Simons never allows his face to be shown in publications so this was to take the place of a profile photo.

CONCEPT: "The idea was to capture the feeling of the early German/Chicago Techno scene; the vibe of the early 1990s underground Techno sound and to mix it with late 1980s – early-1990s surfer gear. I was careful not to do a parody or retro style, but rather to pick up on the feeling and spirit of the scene and movement."

SOLUTION: For the invite: "To ignore all preconceptions of the 'Raf Simons' image as well as to try to imagine where he was going without seeing it. I was only given two key words to help capture the feeling he was going for."
For the portrait: "The Colette article was based on the horoscopes of different designers and artists so along with my interpretation of Mr. Simons himself, I mixed in motifs relevant to his star sign: Capricorn."

LESSON: "Since I admire what Raf Simons does and have followed his work, I was careful not to think in terms of what he might like or do a piece which I thought might please him. I was approached because they wanted my work and thought it would fit with his, so doing it any other way would not have been what the client wanted."

SEVEN NEW YORK

IN ASSOCIATION WITH

SYNDICATE

PRESENT

RAF SIMONS

AUTUMN / WINTER 2004
PRESENTATION AND AFTER-PARTY

SUNDAY   FEBRUARY 8TH   2004

9PM

MARQUEE 289 TENTH AVE
BETWEEN 26TH AND 27TH

COCKTAILS BY PEARL VODKA

AUDIO BY

MICHEL GAUBERT
AND
SPECIAL GUESTS

DESIGN BY KENZO MINAMI

PUBLIC RELATIONS BY SYNDICATE 212 204 7926   SYNDICATE
RSVP BY SATURDAY FEB 7TH TO : RSVPRaf@syndicate-ny.com

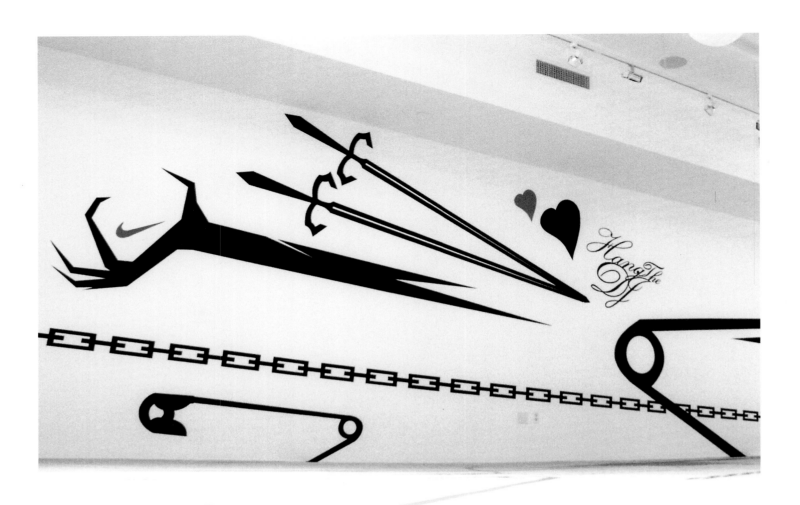

NIKE RECONSTRUCT

CLIENT: Nike Gallery Space, New York, USA.

BRIEF: "Nike picked me as the first artist to paint the whole of the new Nike Gallery Space that they had just opened. They basically let me paint what I wanted."

CONCEPT: "Since the theme of the show was 'Nike Reconstruct', I wanted the piece – which took up the entire space – to be constructed out of separate pieces that used to be one whole. So basically, I started out designing the piece first then took it apart and reassembled the pieces by connecting them with a safety pin motif in various sizes. So this piece only exists in the 'remixed' form as its 'original'."

SOLUTION: The painting covered two walls, the floor and part of the ceiling. The main challenge for Minami was getting the job done in time. "Painting the entire space in eight nights, as I was working on some commercial work at the time during the day was hard. The space was about 40ft long, 11ft high and 30ft wide. Perfect planning was crucial due to the complexity of the painting and having to fit all the pieces together. I had absolutely no time to lose since I was already cutting my sleep down to three hours per day."

LESSON: "The key to success lies in the planning."

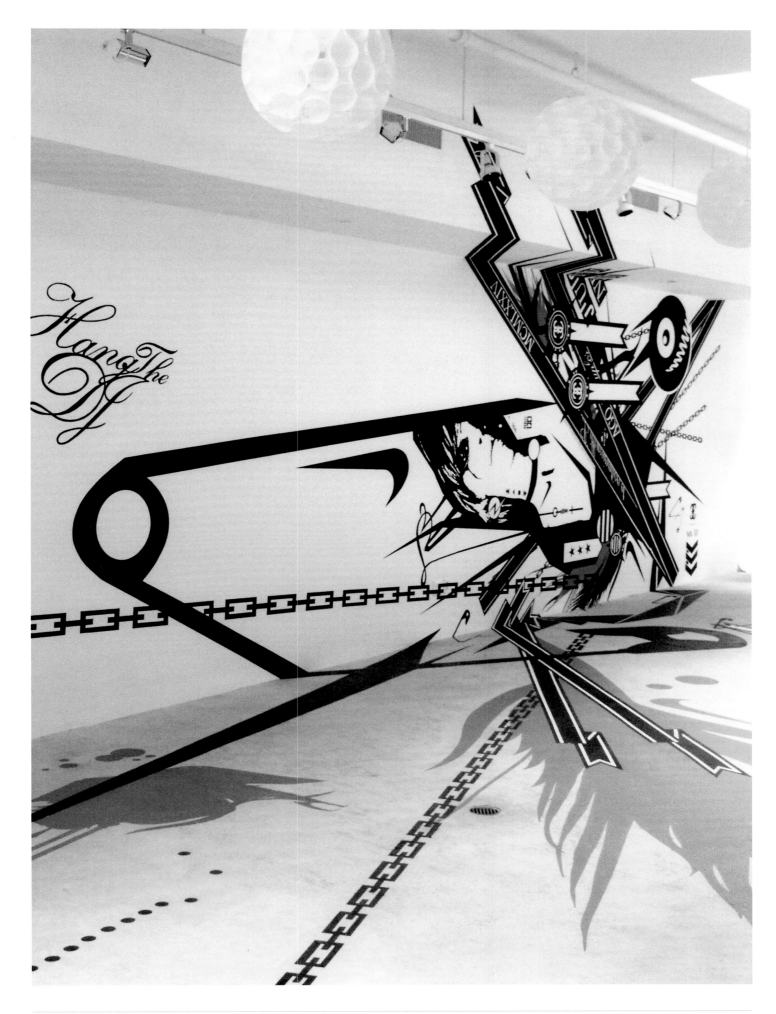

GREIGE

LOCATION: Berlin, Germany

PROFILE: Rupert Kopp, Tammo Claassen and Mark Kiessling all studied design together at the FH Köln in Germany. They later moved to Berlin where they founded Greige in 2001. Areas of interest include; corporate communication, product design, interior design and digital solutions.

MISSION: Kiessling, Kopp and Claassen don't simply perceive their job to be that of knocking functions into form, they are also interested in putting their work in a cultural context. "We take up impulses, work them into projects and then put the entire result back into cultural circulation." By working in a wide variety of fields, they try to keep their work interesting for themselves and maintain the quality of their results. "Consequent, on the line, reduced to the essentials and focused on new materials and techniques."

CLIENTS: Zumtobel Staff, Artforum Berlin, Y-3 Adidas Sportstyle, Dussmann, Bertelssmann, Lexikon Verlag, Marc O'Polo.

ART FORUM BERLIN

CLIENT: Galerie für Gegenwartskunst / Barbara Claassen-Schmal, Bremen, Germany.

BRIEF: To design and produce an exhibition display for the gallery at the Berlin Art Forum, with a budget of only €500 and two days building time.

CONCEPT: At the Art Forum the year before, Greige had designed a display for the gallery called "Cardboard Room". This time around they wanted to go for a "white cube" feel from floor to ceiling — "a clean room for art".

SOLUTION: They spent two days cutting and sewing a white fabric called "Tyvek" to line the booth with and, "to get that look as if the whole booth was dressed in its best clothes". The result, they claim, was a great success; it was "the brightest, most visited space" in the whole art fair.

LESSON: As a result of all this hard work with a small, borrowed sewing machine, Greige were commissioned to come up with a concept for a much larger, 300 sq. metre, lounge/reading room for the Art Forum the following year.

Photo: Mark Kiessling, Greige

Photo: Christoph Voy, www.ishot-berlin.de

Photo: Christoph Voy, I shot studios / Berlin, www.ishot-berlin.de

3DELUXE
GRAPHICS

LOCATION: Wiesbaden, Germany

PROFILE: 3deluxe is an interdisciplinary design company formed in 1992 which consists of around 20 individuals trained in art, interior design, graphics, media design, product design and architecture. The original three founders of the company: Nick Schweiger (interior design), Andreas Lauhoff and Stephan Lauhoff (graphic design) graduated in 1992 from the Fachhochschule Wiesbaden. They were joined by Dieter Brell (interior design) a little later. There are eight people from this group working as graphic designers. They operate under the name of 3deluxe graphics.

MISSION: "In many of our projects we aspire to strip printed representations of the traditional two-dimensional status they are usually accorded. We are interested in graphically defining all three dimensions. As a result, graphic design becomes a spatial experience, and the third dimension becomes the medium conveying information."

CLIENTS: CocoonClub, Fanatic, Burton, Carhart, Zanders Feinpapiere, VW, ADIDAS, E.ON Energie, BASF.

COCOONCLUB

CLIENT: CocoonClub, Frankfurt, Germany

BRIEF: To design the graphics for a club and two restaurants, in collaboration with an interdisciplinary team of designers and architects that redefines what is understood as contemporary club culture.

CONCEPT: "The focus was on the dialogue between music and design philosophies, the graphic design had to be part of the whole philosophy of the club. Architecture, graphic design, Internet, multimedia and communication all had to speak the same language. The CocoonClub was conceived as an avant-garde field of experimentation where space and perception could be transformed. The idea was to create a constantly changing semi-virtual atmosphere."

SOLUTION: "3deluxe graphics produced the interior graphics, corporate design, print and multimedia projections for the CocoonClub, the Micro Club restaurant and the Silk Bed restaurant."

LESSON: "That the co-operation of different disciplines can result in one vibrant concept for club music, high-quality restaurants and design."

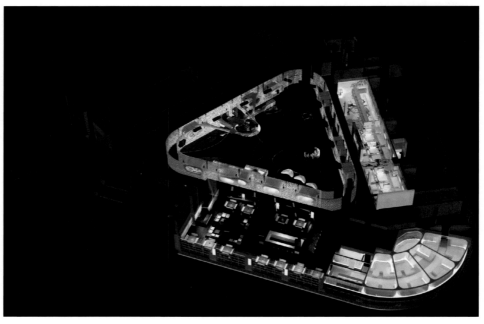

OUTPUT

LOCATION: Nottingham, UK

PROFILE: Output is a design studio formed in the summer of 2002 by three designers; Rob Coke, who studied graphic design and typography at the London College of Printing; Dan Moore, who studied Fine Art at Derby University; and Ian Hambleton who did Communication Studies at Nottingham Trent University and takes care of the creative marketing and PR projects for the company and clients. They produce a wide range of work; interpreting music, fashion, PR, broadcasting, interior space and the arts into visual communication for print and on-screen.

MISSION: "Our primary aim is to give our clients the ability to communicate clearly, creatively and effectively. Beyond this we are especially interested in adding value to the message through its visual interpretation. We have a very direct approach. We like to be designing constantly, sharing ideas and learning from each project that we do. We believe that the best work comes through a process of research and development and not always knowing what the project will look like before it's started."

CLIENTS: BBC Radio 1, BBC 1Xtra, Mantis Recordings, Marine Parade Records, MTV Europe, Onfire, Shine Communications, Solution Footwear, Technique Recordings.

TEA FACTORY

CLIENT: The Tea Factory Bar and Kitchen, Liverpool, UK

BRIEF: Design an identity and print campaign that reflects the specific location of the bar and appeals to a wide audience without being "over designed".

CONCEPT: "The restaurant is situated in a renovated tea warehouse near the docks in Liverpool – an important trading centre in British history. We wanted to create an identity which reflected this history; which looked as if it was a discovered part of the building rather than imposed upon it. We also recognised that the identity needed to appeal to a modern audience."

SOLUTION: "The logotype itself is a simple, industrial-looking typeface set in two ways to create a regular and compact version. A secondary stamp device like a franking mark was created and added to the logo. The position of the stamp mark is random and stamps were made up, to be used on site to create an interaction with the identity. The centrepiece of the bar is an eight-metre-wide mural of a world map displaying tea-shipping routes, with a stylised topographic diagram showing information on world tea production and consumption. The world map graphic also functions as a secondary identity for the bar and is used on menus, posters, flyers and other ephemera."

LESSON: "We learned how important it is to spend time researching a project thoroughly to create a design solution with depth as well as visual appeal."

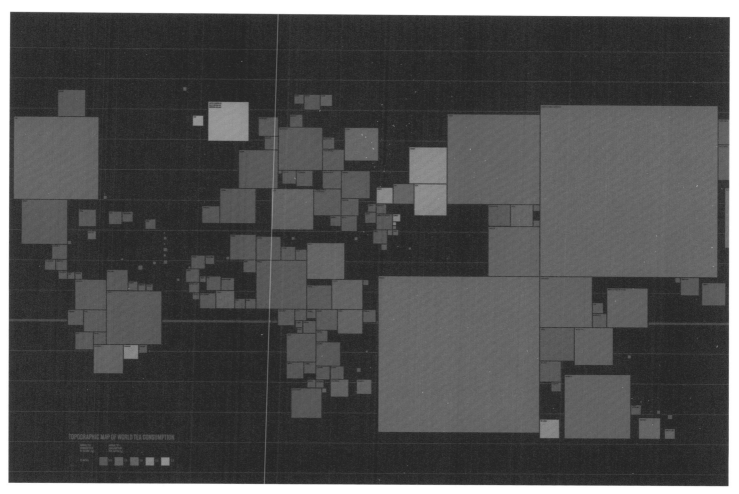

TOPOGRAPHIC MAP OF WORLD TEA CONSUMPTION

PRECURSOR

LOCATION: London, UK

PROFILE: Precursor is a multi-disciplinary design company and was formed in July 2002 by Directors; Chris Angelkhov, Noah Harris and Tim Swift. Their output is split between design for print and design for the moving image. Their work is regularly featured in the design press and their short films "Anomaly" and "Quietus" have been screened at the onedotzero and resfest film festivals.

MISSION: "Our process is about good ideas, innovative and stylish graphic design. We operate a small studio with a focused team and have extensive experience in on- and off-screen branding, design for print, moving-image design and art direction. We devote time to personal, experimental projects where we can develop new techniques and try out new ideas, which then inform our commercial work."

CLIENTS: MTV Europe (top 20 chart graphics package), Channel 4 ("Always On" promo for Channel4.com), Bent (music video and posters, Ministry of Sound Recordings), S.I.Futures (music video, Novamute Records), 4i Group (Orange business commercials), Si Begg (artwork and press photography, Novamute Records).

19:20 BAR

CLIENT: 19:20 Bar, London, UK.

BRIEF: Create an image for a 19-metre-long, curved wall in the upstairs pool bar. "19:20 has been our local watering hole for many years. We spent many an hour propping up the bar and eyeing up the vast canvas upon which we would unleash our work."

CONCEPT: "This upstairs bar houses several pool tables and people go there to play pool. We created a fictional battleground between warring factions – 'spots' and 'stripes' surrounding an iconic world map."

SOLUTION: "We did the work in early 2003 but the client was uneasy about putting it up as Britain and America were about to unleash themselves onto Iraq and the military references – although tongue in cheek – are obvious. The final piece was eventually installed in October and is a montage of photographic imagery and graphic elements; the piece was printed onto digital wallpaper and applied directly to the wall."

LESSON: "Working on this sort of scale is not something we do very often. Much of our work is moving image intended for the TV screen. Levels of detail are very different at this scale. With hindsight there are some elements that probably could have been designed differently. The beauty of it is though, that when we or the client get bored of looking at it, we can tear it down and produce something new."

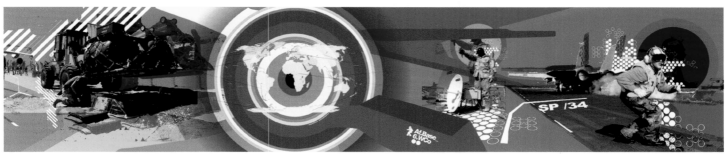

DAVINIA TAYLOR WEDDING INVITATION

CLIENT: Davinia Taylor, UK

BRIEF: "Create a stand out, unique set of wedding stationery for a high-profile wedding. The client was quite particular about what they didn't want. The invite was to land on the doormat of lots of celebs so it had to have impact – it had to be luxurious."

CONCEPT: "There is not really an 'idea' as such behind this piece, it is much more about the materials used and the simplicity and elegance of the finished project."

SOLUTION: "The main invitation is a square of stainless steel with radius corners, the floral pattern is laser-cut and the typographic information is acid-etched from the surface. This is housed, along with a screen-printed, fold-out information sheet, in a bespoke white case. The couple's names are foil blocked in silver. The whole pack is very tactile and although quite cold at first glance, has quite a feminine feel."

LESSON: "We'd never worked with metal before so that was an interesting process. We often use screen printing and blocking in our print work so there was little to learn there."

MTV HIJACK

CLIENT: MTV International, London, UK

BRIEF: "The initial brief was very open, possibly even a little vague; MTV wanted to find a way of summing up the creative attitude of the company, and creating a 'source of inspiration' for MTV creative departments around the world. The second part of the brief was to put this theory into practice and create a new on-air look based on the big idea of 'MTVness'."

CONCEPT: "We bounced a lot of ideas around for this one and with the brief being so loose it was not a straightforward process. The idea we eventually settled on was 'hijack'. MTV is about music – it's a music channel – but it is also an icon of youth culture. This concept of hijacking is not only prevalent in popular culture at the moment – bootlegging, fly-posting, customising clothing, graffiti – also daytime radio is full of one-time pirate radio artists and crews. Hijacking is also to be found elsewhere – Chapman Brothers' Goya paintings, Christo's large-scale artworks, Adbusters, even plastic surgery falls into our definition. Of course hijack is a very taboo word now too; it has powerful meanings and is relatively unexpected when used in this way."

SOLUTION: "We pitched for the project against several companies. Strangely enough another company, Hi-ReS!, came up with a strikingly similar idea, using the word 'Hijack' with many of the same influences and points of reference we had used, so the project was awarded to both companies with Precursor handling the new on-air look. The concept gave us a lot of freedom from a design perspective; we wanted the on-air look to be quite free and based around the DIY ethic of many of our points of reference for the initial idea. First, we shot everyday scenes on 16mm film – a laundrette, a library and a 1970s Plaxton school bus. We then tracked the scenes and hijacked them with graphic elements mixing traditional methods such as frame-by-frame animation and stencil-sprayed logos with 3D elements."

LESSON: "Because the project was briefed in such a way as to have two distinct parts, we approached it in differently to how we normally would with a channel brand. We had no real preconceived ideas about the end result. The concept we came up with meant that there was a lot of experimentation and many accidents made their way into the final work. The budget for the project was not immense so we had to be quite creative when shooting the initial scenes; we ended up shooting the bus using a skateboard dragged across a door on top of the seats, there was no other way we could get the shot without putting a crane through the front window and we just couldn't afford that."

In the land of fairytales, designers would study and develop their talents at college, hone them and gain experience by working at an agency and then, shortly after heading off into the real world, hook a career-defining jewel of a job that would launch their reputation on the international stage and have clients queuing up to pop cheques in their bank account for every little sketch that left their desktop. Is this pure fantasy or a plausible scenario? By what yardstick do designers measure their own success and how does it come about?

The "big break": that magical big job that gets your name out there and starts the commissions flooding in. Is that how it really happens?
LOBO: "In our case it was probably a sequence of breaks. It was a very long process that took about five years of hard work. Sometimes we had bad patches that took all the endurance we could muster to get over. So success is probably more related to endurance than timing."
FRANÇOIS CHALET: "My big break came with my illustrations and animations for MTV Alarm in 1998; things took of from there."
JONATHAN BARNBROOK: "I don't like the idea of the 'big break' to be quite honest – it sounds too pop star. Work builds up over a long period of time and usually comes from word of mouth. You work for somebody and they are hopefully very happy with the result and tell someone else. I think people who suddenly come on to the scene can fade quite quickly."

Is winning a commission from Coca-Cola, Adidas, Nike, Levi's or whatever the big break that all designers dream of?
JONATHAN BARNBROOK: "I wouldn't work for any of those companies. I've turned down Coca-Cola and I wouldn't work for Nike or Adidas because of what they represent and what they have been implicated in. They should be designers' nightmares not their dreams."
FULGURO: "It must be hard to say no to Coca-Cola. It is so good with ice. We are sure it must be 'cool' to work for them, but it is certainly not a 'must'."
FRANÇOIS CHALET: "If I can do my own thing with them then yes! Of course it would be ideal if you could do your own thing, have it shown worldwide and you got fame and money for it. The contradiction is that the more people you need to communicate with, the flatter the message or the design needs to be. It is therefore highly unlikely that I would be able to do something really wicked for them, but it's worth trying!"

What are the pitfalls and pleasures of working for multinationals?
JONATHAN BARNBROOK: "The ethical issue is the biggest problem; it is difficult to know where responsibility stops really. Is doing an advert for alcohol bad? Is doing an advert for a car bad? These things in isolation are not the problem, the problem is the structure of the society that is promoting them. It's very difficult to know when to say yes or no."
FRANÇOIS CHALET: "I've worked for Mitsubishi, MTV and a couple of other big companies. Mostly they pay better – except MTV."
KASIA KORCZAK: "Cultural misunderstandings are the elements to be aware of while working with multinationals. From my experience every culture has their own way of evaluating work, different aesthetics and method of working."

Are they the new Medicis?
LOBO: "The entities that hold power have always sponsored artists to produce work that displays themselves as the main subjects. So one can say that just as in the past when the church or monarchs were in that position, today we have empowered corporations."
JONATHAN BARNBROOK: "The point in the end is to maximise profit to shareholders. If they pay for a basketball court, they do it specifically to get their logo on it as part of the cool culture of the street, there's no other reason. They are trying to sell people the same product over and over again so they have to change the form of it as often as they can and it is exploitative in that sense. I don't really understand why graphic designers are so eager to work for such companies. Perhaps it represents some kind of freedom or experimentation, but it's only experimentation within the realm of it functioning to sell their product to people."

Have you only made it when you have an MTV animation trophy in your portfolio or are big name clients basically irrelevant?
LOBO: "We do have MTV projects in our portfolio, and it's not irrelevant, but just as important as many of our other projects."
KASIA KORCZAK: "It's irrelevant. MTV is not a measure anymore. Maybe it used to be years ago but these days I doubt anybody really cares.

You don't measure a good creative by the clients they have but by the work they do."

FRANÇOIS CHALET: "Yes, it's true, that lots of people think that MTV is quite a trophy. It gives prestige and when you have worked for them you can most probably be used for campaigns aimed at young people. If I'm doing a job for a bank though, then MTV is not so important."

When you get chosen by a multinational brand to do work for local campaigns are you just being used? Is it a parasitical exploitation of your pioneering experimentation or is it a symbiotic relationship?

FULGURO: "It was a new experience; there were very good relationships with young and dynamic people but the work was not very experimental. They were not really that interested in out true work, it had more to do with geography."

LOBO: "We like to think of ourselves not as artists, but as artisans. That said, the relationship would have to be symbiotic, because we trade our craft for a fee. We have to fulfil both the client's expectations, and our own quality standards. This kind of thinking can be very naïve. If you think someone is exploiting you, why accept the job?"

KASIA KORCZAK: "I think it is symbiotic. The client and myself are fully aware of what we are getting into. Even if the client goes to a designer for what s/he has recently done, and often just wants a reproduction of that, the designer is fully aware of this. If not, s/he is naïve. There is no conspiratorial exploitation or 'us versus them' to it."

FRANÇOIS CHALET: "Symbiotic is a bit of an exaggeration. They have what I want (money) and I have what they want (style). The only remaining issue is how much I have to round off the edges. If I have to compromise too much then I don't want to do it."

What about getting a big break from an arts organisation like a big gallery or theatre? How does cultural work differ from corporate?

FULGURO: "Cultural work is more experimental, more free. Culture doesn't have to please everybody. It is a more affirmative way of working. A breath of fresh air in fact."

JONATHAN BARNBROOK: "There's no difference. There's still a corporate structure and you still have the same political relationships between people in an arts organisation as you do in a company. But I suppose there still is the feeling that you are trying to do something positive by promoting art. I don't think there is any point in just working for arts organisations or museums. If you want your work to be influential then you obviously have to go out into the wide world."

LOBO: "In cultural work you don't depend on anyone's approval. That is a huge difference from commercial work, where you rarely do whatever you think is right. But both things differ a lot in nature. But then again, we're not artists, Lobo is a design studio. That doesn't mean we wouldn't display our work in a gallery, but it wouldn't make us artists."

KASIA KORCZAK: "Graphic design is an applied art after all. Whether it's advertising shoes or a play it is still a commercial task the designer has to face. Nevertheless the way of working for art-based or commercial clients can be very different. The 'art' audience usually has a higher visual education, enabling you to experiment more. But then again, I must admit that being able to create good work for a commercial client is a difficult and admirable challenge too. There are totally different factors you have to focus on, maybe even more difficult as there are lots of restrictions. When you succeed, you surely deserve a lot of respect."

FRANÇOIS CHALET: "That is a difficult question, because cultural jobs have changed enormously in the last few years and are more and more defined by market rules."

Who would be your dream client?

JONATHAN BARNBROOK: "Somebody who's doing something decent in the world, which is why we tend to work with museums and institutions. We haven't done it yet but we would like to work with more political organisations like the United Nations. Part of the problem with graphic design is that so much of what you are saying is pointless – I would rather have some messages which mean something to people."

FULGURO: "Apple – to redesign Mac OS X and get free computers."

KASIA KORCZAK: "Of course the ideal clients are those who are just starting out. There is nothing more challenging then working on a project from scratch. This is when you have the biggest freedom and you are the one who decides on a visual identity."

DOES SIZE MATTER? DOES A BIG BUDGET MAKE A DIFFERENCE TO CREATIVE QUALITY?

LOBO: "Usually the more money that's at stake, the bigger the risks are. This can put the client under pressure to avoid taking risks. But there are exceptions, and we hope to work with those."

KASIA KORCZAK: "Most creatives are prepared to put in more if they get something in return. That can for example be creative freedom, a new experience or interesting collaboration."

FRANÇOIS CHALET: "You can design an incredibly sexy button badge or create an amazing MTV campaign. The difference is that it is probably much easier to make the incredibly sexy button badge because less money, pressure and politics are involved."

JONATHAN BARNBROOK: "Yes and no; much of the most exciting work has been done on A4-photocopied sheets. Think of the punk movement and fanzines and that kind of thing. There's a saying that the best fruit comes from the hardest pruned trees, so restrictions to design can be very good for producing exciting work. Obviously it is sometimes nice to have a big budget but it is not always the best thing – it can make a piece of work decadent as well."

HI-RES!

LOCATION: London, UK

PROFILE: "We are currently two artistic directors, two designers, two programmers and one studio manager, and sometimes one to two interns. Alexandra Jugovic and Florian Schmitt are the artistic directors and owners of the company, which they founded in London in 1999. Jugovic and Schmitt both studied together in Germany at the Hochschule für Gestaltung in Offenbach and graduated in December 1995. After their studies, they worked in a film production house (Anzilotti and Münzing, later Inmotion AG) on an in-house record-label: Jugovic as art director and Schmitt as 3D artist, visual effect supervisor and later director on various music videos and commercials. They both enjoyed the experience, and the relative creative freedom but nevertheless decided to go freelance and set up their own company together.

MISSION: "Hi-Res! is an independent creative consultancy, new media and design studio in London. We are an international team, representing six countries. Everything we do is built on ideas and finding the most creative solution for every product and medium. And about having as much fun as possible while doing so."

CLIENTS: HBO, USA; Lions Gate Entertainment, USA; MTV International, UK; Dentsu, Japan; Mitsubishi Motors, Japan; Lexus Motors, USA; SONY Computer Entertainment Europe, UK.

THE DREAMERS

CLIENT: Hanway Films, London, UK

BRIEF: Create a website for Bernardo Bertolucci's film "Dreamers", a film about sexual and political awakening in France in 1968.

CONCEPT: The film depicts a ménage á trois between a young American exchange student and a French brother and sister set against the stark background of the 1968 riots in Paris. "The aim of the website was to retell parts of the film but altogether in a dreamlike way, as if you had seen the film and were dreaming about it, at times drawing linear parallels to the present and mixing up the linear narrative of the film."

SOLUTION: "Just like the film, the site is set entirely in a vast Parisian apartment and allows you to enter the various rooms to get a glimpse of parts of the story. The further you progress into the site, the more messy the apartment becomes and the more frequently the outside world of political riots intrudes on the story until at last you 'awaken' slightly confused about what was real and what was a dream."

STYLE LAB

CLIENT: Diesel Stylelab, Italy

BRIEF: "We had no brief from the client, just the fashion images and some graphics that were used in the collection."

CONCEPT: The project was inspired originally by the lyrics to the Dead Kennedys' song "California über Alles":
"Now it is 1984
Knock knock at your front door
It's the suede/denim secret police
They have come for your uncool niece..."

SOLUTION: "We developed a Java applet which converts images into line drawings, evolving over time and then wrote it as new code for Shockwave. The result is an image which hints at the underlying source image, but looks more like a torn net-stocking, which is one of the metaphors we chose for the punk-themed collection; the mesh is a metaphor for the Web itself. Another aim was to create an audio-ambience which is calm and dulcet, paired with very intense spoken-word content and distorted guitars."

LESSON: "As we were not able to get permission to use Jello Biafra's lyrics we chose the poem "Tale" from "Illuminations" by Arthur Rimbaud instead – transforming the site into a weird and disturbing fairytale."

MASSIVE ATTACK

CLIENT: Virgin Records, London, UK

BRIEF: Create a website to coincide with the launch of Massive Attack's fourth album: "100th Window'.

CONCEPT: "The site was designed to have two faces, innocence and experience, a flat site and an immersive site. One would communicate facts, the other would use the facts and put them in context."

SOLUTION: "One way we did this was by using positional data from tour locations and super-imposing live earthquake data onto a world map. How close can they be to disaster, or using live stock market data to see how the political climate influences the stock market. The experience part of the site was always meant to be hidden away to a certain extent; sometimes surfacing, always lurking beneath the flat information, sometimes you would have to uncover it. 99 windows are closed and the 100th window has been left open for you to enter."

LESSON: "It is a system that is being influenced from outside (Massive Attack's submissions in the form of visuals, audio, video) and inside (news images and pictures pulled by us through Google's image search into the site). The factor of unpredictability and surprise, which is pre-determined in so many of our sites was not in our own hands anymore."

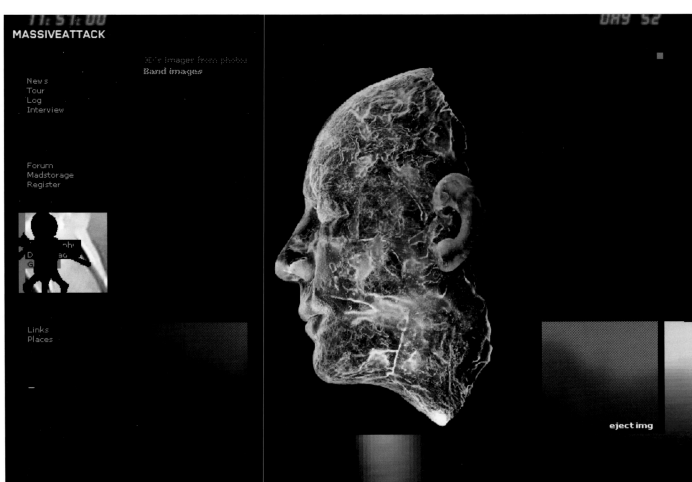

MASSIVEATTACK

It's images from photos
Band images

News
Tour
Log
Interview

Forum
Madstorage
Register

Links
Places

eject img

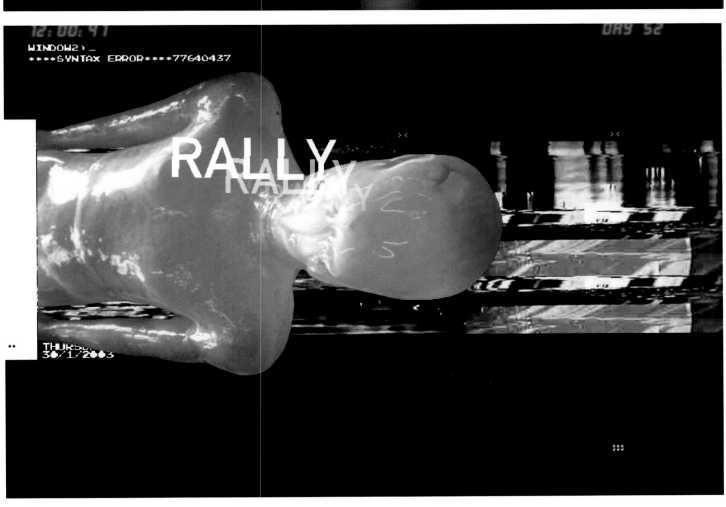

WINDOW2 › _
****SYNTAX ERROR****77640437

RALLY
RALLY

THURSDAY
30/1/2003

888

LOBO

LOCATION: Sao Paulo, Brazil

PROFILE: "Lobo started nine years ago with three guys, two of which are still partners to this day. We started out very small, for fun and to do a little work together. The first few years were a real struggle, but after we joined Vetor Zero crew (a big 3D and post-production company in Brazil), things started to flow. The team comes from all over Brazil, plus a couple of adopted Europeans. We also come from all sorts of different backgrounds, but the majority of the crew graduated in design and architecture. Lobo mainly creates animation and design for TV, advertising, film and fashion."

MISSION: "We try to avoid repeating ourselves and to keep exploring new ground. As we work for very diverse clients and projects, there is never a single style to fit them all. We always have to find what's right for each project, instead of trying to fit the same approach to everything."

CLIENTS: "We usually work for TV networks and agencies. Some of the most recent are Cartoon Network, Nickelodeon, VH1, Anime Network, Viva Channel, Panasonic, Subaru, Toyota, and Diesel."

JUM NAKAO

CLIENT: Jum Nakao, Sao Paulo, Brazil

BRIEF: "The fashion designer Jum Nakao asked us to create the textile prints and the catalogue for his spring/summer collection."

CONCEPT: "The goal was to translate his ideas for the actual clothes into graphics without changing the meaning and concept of the collection but instead reinforcing it. The difficulty was to accurately interpret what the client was looking for along the way. Since we got involved very early on in the process, we started to have our own ideas about what the graphics should be and how they should work. Jum wanted the collection to refer to kitsch, but he also wanted us to come up with a contemporary interpretation of it."

SOLUTION: "The 'future-kitsch' concept: trying to reinterpret kitsch through the eye of contemporary techniques. The saturated colours, the somewhat obvious flowers and flamingos, turned out original and pretty when modelled in 3D."

LESSON: "This was our first big project for print. Being more used to working in electronic media, it was nice to learn how to translate our design ideas into a different medium. This is knowledge that we have absorbed, and will certainly use in future projects."

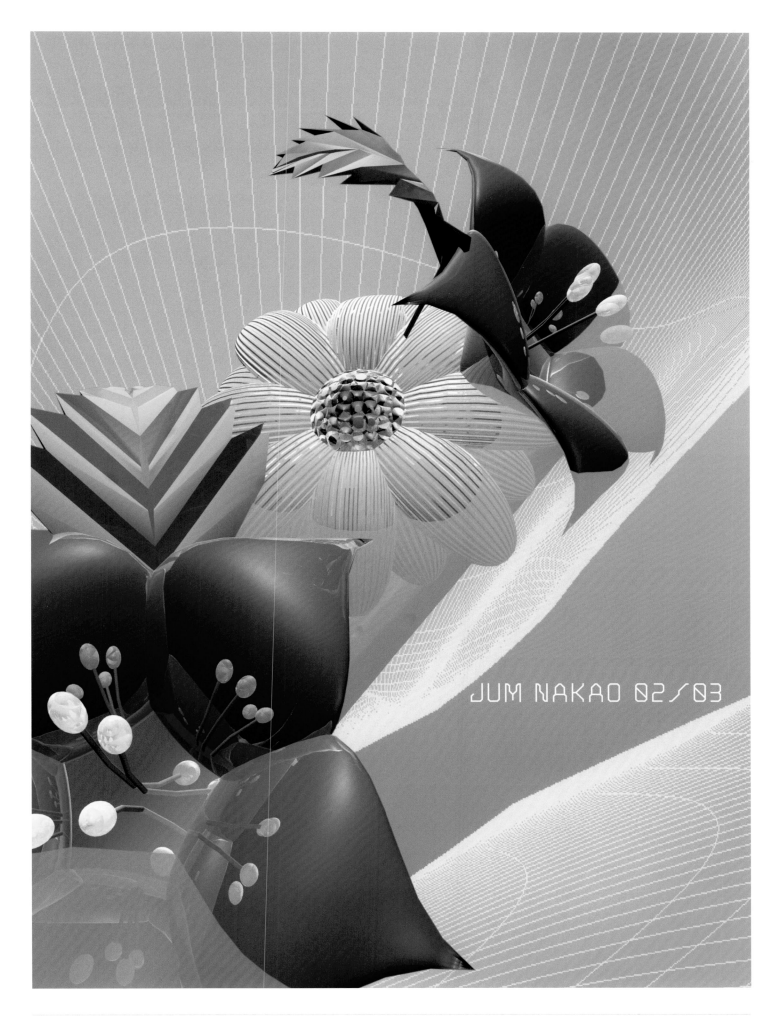

JUM NAKAO 02/03

LOST PARADISE

CLIENT: Diesel, Molvena, Italy

BRIEF: "Diesel contacted us to animate the textile prints of their spring/summer collection. The goal was to make it look interesting and to add a mystery mood."

CONCEPT: "The theme was 'Lost Paradise'. Literature and film references concerning pirates and shipwrecks; searching for treasure, or a character lost on a faraway island that he's forced to explore. All these provided a backbone for the narrative. Thanks to the schedule we had plenty of time to think about the project and figure out an appropriate concept for the piece. At first we found it very hard to develop the guidelines for it, but after stapling the textile prints to our office walls and staring at them for months, it finally came together."

SOLUTION: "The result was a five-minute video for Diesel's promotional DVD and two cuts for TV. It is a piece that uses several different animation techniques. It doesn't conform to current industry standards, yet is a fine piece of marketing that also entertains the public in an unusual way."

LESSON: "Having fun is the key to success."

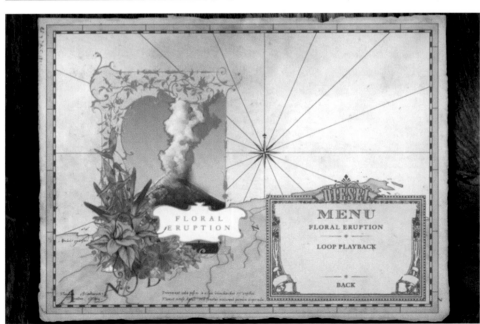

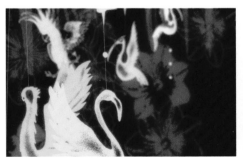

DISCO ROUT

CLIENT: Ghostly International Music, Ann Arbor, Michigan, USA

BRIEF: "The record label Ghostly International asked us to do a music video for the track 'Disco Rout' by the band Legowelt."

CONCEPT: "To try and make a 3D piece which had the flat look of poster art. We really wanted to do something inspired by the Swiss and French tourism posters and adverts from the 1930s so this video seemed like a good opportunity."

SOLUTION: "It was our first work that was created entirely on Maya running on a Macintosh platform. It took us six months to finish it. The video is really a motion graphics piece in the sense that it is completely inspired by illustrations. You could take many stills from the spot and they would look just as good as posters; it's moving design."

LESSON: "Creating a music video piece that everybody likes and feels happy about is hard work."

STATE

LOCATION: London, UK

PROFILE: "There are two directors at State: Mark Hough and Philip O'Dwyer. We share our studio with our main client, onedotzero. We graduated with MAs in Communication Design from Central Saint Martins College, London in December 1995 and set up State in August 1997. In between, Mark did internships at Tomato, Nick Bell Design, and Doublespace in New York and Philip did an internship at Wired magazine, London. These were useful experiences because they gave us an insight into how design groups of different sizes and natures differ, plus the opportunity to work on commercial pieces while still being in a college environment."

MISSION: "We work across the boundaries of print, moving image and interactive media, striving to make functional, beautiful objects, whether physical or digital. We believe that the most exciting results are to be found by expressing the essential nature of content."

CLIENTS: Sony Computer Entertainment Europe, (SCEE), onedotzero, MTV, Panasonic, Toyota, the Barbican Gallery.

BEST OF 2003

CLIENT: MTV Networks Europe, London, UK

BRIEF: Create a ten-second title sequence for the thirteen "Best of 2003" programmes.

CONCEPT: "To show a year in ten seconds without directly alluding to music videos."

SOLUTION: "The final product was a series of ten-second animations used to package the thirteen 'Best of 2003' shows on MTV. It was created using Lightwave, Illustrator and After Effects and takes the form of an armchair sliding through the four seasons in one day."

LESSON: "Originally a pitch, this was a small trial piece to test combining still images inspired by print and fully-rendered 3D pieces in a seamless way. We found that with only a few elements and carefully chosen colours we could achieve the desired result. The whole piece was created in-house in a week, Jude Greenaway composed the audio accompaniment."

DIXONBAXI

LOCATION: London, UK

PROFILE: Simon Dixon graduated from York College, England in 1990 and Aporva Baxi from Middlesex University in 1994. Dixon joined a UK design team and opened several studios in the UK and the USA while Baxi worked with several large UK design teams, as well as in the USA and Australia before they settled down and formed a partnership together in London in 2002.

MISSION: dixonbaxi call themselves "designers who also direct". Dixon defines their partnership as, "a design practice that offers design, art direction and directing with strong ideas, content and execution. We also have a lot of experience with large companies and so understand the logistics of handling and managing large projects. Together, we have a very broad experience of different types of design and TV projects, so our combined knowledge helps to make the most from each idea. We also have very high production values. None of this is unique, but the combination gives us a little niche that we are comfortable with".

CLIENTS: Microsoft, Sony, Adidas, Intel, Fox Networks, MTV UK, ESPN, DLJ Direct, General Motors, CNET, MTV2, Audi, VH1, Nike, Reebok, Amstel, Comedy Central, Channel 10, Ashford.com, Sybase, Ford, Fox 8, Lucas Arts, Columbia Tristar, Rotovision, Drug Free America, Tanner Krolle.

MTV2

CLIENT: MTV2, UK, London

BRIEF: Reposition and redesign the MTV2 channel. "To achieve a better connection with the MTV2 audience and increase ratings. The audience of young, male rock fans don't like to be sold messages by big brands. The challenge was finding a way to communicate with them without being condescending or irrelevant."

CONCEPT: "We took ideas, messages and content directly from the audience via web chatrooms and put it on the screen. For the initial presentation we created a series of paintings to represent the world of an MTV2 viewer. Paint, concrete, flyers and signs ripped from walls all went into a collage. This led us to create designs as immediate and direct as the cultural references they tapped into."

SOLUTION: "A solution of animating idents that used typography as a bold and confident voice. The design system is both flexible and updateable to keep the channel alive and fresh with new ideas."

LESSON: "Not to talk down to or sell to the audience."

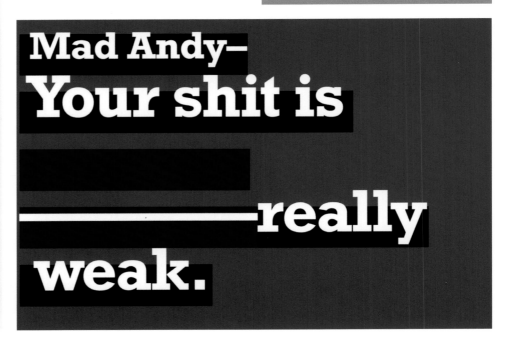

VH1

CLIENT: VH1, London, UK

BRIEF: To create a fresh take on the VH1 logo use and look for this UK TV channel.

CONCEPT: "We needed to add some glamour, energy and impact." They approached the channel as a series of graphic patterns representing different moods and tones. "We wanted to look at a treatment that would surprise the audience."

SOLUTION: "Rather than the typical use of images or film to represent the music, we created an animated world of coloured graphic forms. The graphic patterns created a series of hypnotic animations that punctuate the channel content. They arrest the eye, grab attention and generate energy."

LESSON: "That Flash is a good TV animation package."

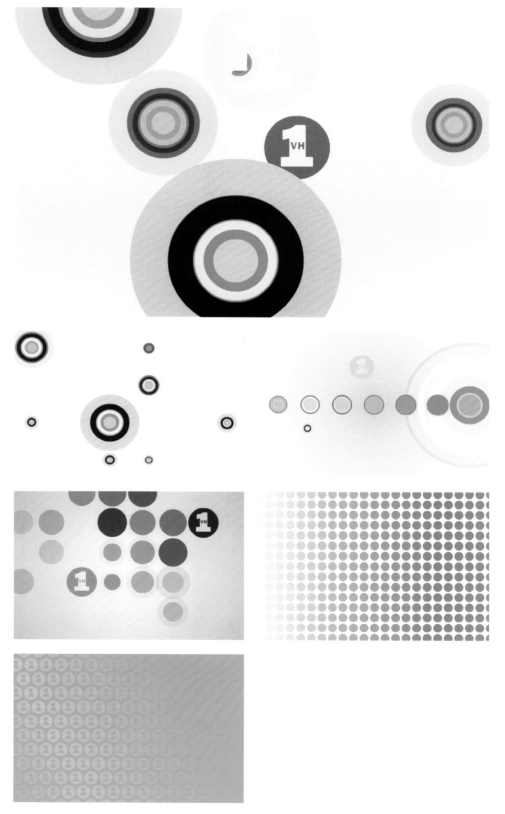

NEUBAU

LOCATION: Berlin, Germany

PROFILE: Born, raised and educated in Austria, Stefan Gandl moved to Berlin in 1996 to do a three-month Corporate Design job and ended up staying. Between 1997 and 1999 he was kept busy doing CI and various projects with Designerdock, a Berlin-based creative personnel recruitment agency. In 2000 he did his first book for Die Gestalten Verlag called DSOS1. He has been operating under the name of Neubau since 2001 and runs his office with one assistant, working with other freelancers as a team when necessary.

MISSION: "Neubau works with paper and Apples", says Gandl. His output covers screen, print, broadcast and, above all, typography.

CLIENTS: MTV USA, MTV Asia, Channel Four UK, Nike, Detroit Underground, Sony Music Germany, Hochschule für Gestaltung und Kunst Zürich (HGKZ), ZKM, Münchner Biennale, Designerdock Europe, The Wire UK, Futurenet Publishing UK.

HEPTAMERON

CLIENT: Media Opera Heptameron by Gerhard E. Winkler. Production: Biennale München 2002, ZKM; Karlsruhe, Germany

BRIEF: This was a collaborative opera project between Lawrence P. Wallen (stage design/concept), Stefan Gandl/Neubau (screen design/concept/motion) and Gerhard Winkler (music/composition), to create interactive theatre.

CONCEPT: "In the interactive world of Heptameron, material from the entire sound sequence and elements of the score and video sequences were translated via sensors and algorithms into real-time and then manipulated. Central to a video design for interactive theatre is the need to clearly show the complex interactive control commands to the audience via the development of a specific visual grammar. In order to help the audience towards this understanding, the complex, non-hierarchical network of the internet seemed to me to provide a good analogy."

SOLUTION: The visual grammar, or language, for the seven worlds of Heptameron were presented in 155 flash movies. "Because the viewer understands the internet as 'user', she/he can enter into the Heptameron world in a playful way. The sound and visual interactivity of Heptameron is an open system with multiple points of entry. There is no beginning or end which means that each performance differs from the others in terms of various combinations of sound, image and scene and therefore remains an 'open whole'."

LESSON: Gandl learned a lot about sensor-controlled motion design within the tight eight-week production schedule and explored a number of new technology applications.

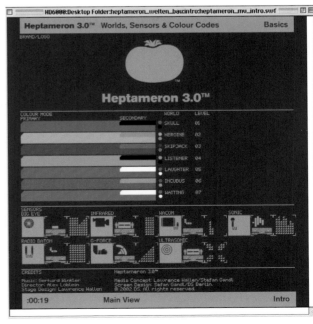

DANCE4

CLIENT: MJW Production, London, UK

BRIEF: First, create a 15–20 second trailer in HD quality for Channel Four and its programme Dance4. Use Atari-esque computer screen aesthetics for the programme opener that relate to the content of the show. Also, create animated chest captions for the two hosts of the programme, Michael Nunn and William Trevitt.

CONCEPT: "To create a game-like feeling by incorporating several fake dance-game logos and introducing the two hosts of the show as 'player one' and 'player two'."

SOLUTION: The 15-second trailer was produced using black and white 2D graphics and various logo animations for non-existing dance-games. The animated Atari-esque chest programmes featured GandI's NB55™ and NBFett™ typefaces for the first time in a TV on-air application.

LESSON: "The challenge was creating a dynamic and convincing visual concept by using these black and white 2D vector graphics. The results produced within the final motion-design broke radically with intro aesthetics of previous shows."

● Dance. Channel 4.
Player 1/Michael Nunn. Host of corresponding programme.
Take dance to the next level. Design and motion made at Neubau/Berlin for MJW Productions Ltd/London.
©2001-2003 Neubau/Berlin.

NB 4DANCE™
HOST A/PLAYER 1/ICON

● Dance. Channel 4.
Logo version "NB Lane". Design and motion made at Neubau/Berlin
for MJW Productions Ltd/London.
Logo ©2001-2003 Neubau.

NB 4DANCE™
LOGO VERSION/SEQUENCE NBLANE™

NB 4DANCE™
LOGO VERSION NBLANE™

NB 4DANCE™
LOGO VERSION/SEQUENCE NBSCRIPT 3D™

NB 4DANCE™
LOGO VERSION NBSCRIPT 3D™

"I believe that all of us have their own individual 'drawer of shame' where we collect the projects which simply did not work out. I try very hard to love that drawer – it is part of my work."
FLORIAN PFEFFER

Should there be a difference between the work that designers do for themselves, for their own amusement and their corporate work – the work that clients commission and pay them to do? Is design that doesn't have a price on its head somehow more virtuous, more creative, purer or better? A designer's attitude to this issue has a lot of bearing on the way they approach all of their work.

For those that view personal and corporate work as two discrete entities, their non-commissioned projects can be a liberating exercise free from the constraints of a brief. These projects represent a wellspring of inspiration and a source of fresh ideas that can hopefully feed back into their corporate work. Maintaining this "yin-yang" approach of parcelling jobs into specific areas also seems to help define boundaries, which in turn helps with the mental organisation and categorisation of one of the most fluid and undefined of disciplines.

KASIA KORCZAK: "I think that underground, cutting edge and corporate are essentially different things and it is very important that they are treated and executed accordingly. Underground (i.e. self-generated work) has a totally different goal and raison d'être than corporate. I believe it is very important for each creative to make sure they do not treat corporate jobs in the same way as underground ones. I think this is usually the reason why many creatives are disappointed after working on corporate jobs as they had the wrong expectations. By this I am not saying that you have to execute commercial jobs without ambition, but each creative has to be aware of the different objectives of each project."

There is a danger, though, that by separating corporate from personal work, the gap between them can become so wide that the designers end up developing Jekyll and Hyde-like tactics to accommodate both strategies. Fanny Khoo says that Flink find it very hard to bridge this gap but still manage to hop across when necessary. "Fortunately, we're very versatile in translating styles from corporate to the more 'cutting edge' and vice versa. Most of the time though we just make a clear divide. It makes life slightly easier."

This separation can also be seen as an implication that corporate work is an area in which one's artistic integrity is compromised. Fons Hickmann makes the point that since corporate design helps a company to communicate, it is an important business factor and as such it is the duty of large corporations to ensure that the staff employed to liase between designers and the company are competent. Otherwise the resulting design will be weakened which is a loss – and compromise – on all sides. "A really difficult situation is when you have to present to people who obviously have no idea of what it is all about. A sort of aesthetic design barbarism rules in certain large corporations, where people with brightly-coloured ties or Louis Vuitton handbags make the corporate design decisions, and that can only lead to disaster."

It is easy to see how a "them and us" situation can develop and clear that the onus is on clients of this kind to ring the changes if they want to get the best from their designers. Perhaps it is better for a designer to consider not making any kind of distinction between their attitude to private and commercial work. For Marco from Vier5, there is no gap between the two and "the work should define the approach", nothing else. The thinking here seems to be that a designer should approach each and every task with the same set of strategies and creative tools regardless of whether they have been invited to design a commercial for washing powder or an installation for a gallery exhibition. Part of this mindset involves not viewing corporate work as a compromise in a creative sense. Kasia Korczak again: "Some of the best graphic design has been corporate. Compromise is part and parcel of the profession. But compromise in the sense of a daily interaction, transaction of services and goods, not ideologically, intellectually or aesthetically."

Since all commissioned work involves compromise to a greater or lesser extent, in terms of the designer having to create work to fit the client's needs, and the client's choice being limited by the options that the designers make available to them, then what could be called "constructive compromise" must be when a solution is reached that the designer feels proud of and the client is happy with. Rilla Alexander from Rinzen: "I don't think corporate work has to mean compromise. I think that's a problem with the way most designers approach things, because they put on their 'corporate' hats and then turn round and put on their 'I'm doing cool stuff' hats. Really the only difference between doing a client job and doing a personal job, is that with a client job you are not the one that sets the parameters. Beyond that, you are basically doing the best job you can for that project. I think you can produce amazing stuff for what seemed at first like the most boring job in the world. If you get excited about something and put the right thinking into it, you can make anything good."

Perhaps the biggest perceived threat to a designer's creative output is the danger of dilution through too much intervention. In extreme cases, this dilution can remove so much life and colour from a designer's original concept that the end result brings more of a sense of loss than of fulfilment. Florian Pfeffer from Jung + Pfeffer: "In our studio history we have had very small and very big 'nightmare clients' as well as very small and very big 'dream clients'. Small/cultural clients sometimes lack professionalism so badly that it becomes impossible to go ahead with a project. I prefer bigger/corporate companies whose goals are more or less clear. On the other hand, big clients tend to discuss everything in committees; this is usually the death of any ambitious design solution."

But isn't commercial design a service industry and isn't it the task of the designer to deliver a required result? Shouldn't their role be part of a team effort towards a particular goal and as such is there any space for outbreaks of ego? This would be easier to answer if designers were selling washing machines or boxes of matches, but they are not, they are selling something that comes from somewhere inside their heads, something that is part of themselves. Because of this, a designer should only accept commissions for jobs that they want to do because if their heads aren't playing ball, then there is no way they can produce a good result. Alternatively they need to develop their own coping strategies. A common tactic is to be firm with the client right from the outset; trusting your own experiences and instincts. "Always listen to your client, then do what you think is right", says Florian Pfeffer; or, "It is important to not always do the design that the client wants, but the one that they need", says Fanny Khoo.

Doing the design that you think works best and then getting the client onside afterwards is also a popular approach: "Simple and beautiful is always the best. What's most important is to persuade the client of this", say Cartlidge Levene. Viewing the client as the "enemy" or in a "them and us" light is also a coping strategy but not necessarily a productive one. Putting up walls and boundaries is fine if it helps, but it is important not to forget that both designer and client are going to have to scale them in order to meet in the middle and complete the job. A little humility and a positive attitude can also have their uses. Then designers like Kasia Korczak can get to say things like: "I've been lucky enough to see some of my clients become collaborators", and you just know that she enjoys her work. Florian Pfeffer makes an interesting final point on the subject of designer/client compromise; namely that, as hinted at above, the clients aren't always the only ones causing obstacles to good creative results. "I always try and bear in mind what the designer Tibor Kalman said in respect to client relations: 'Good clients are smarter than you. Bad clients are dumber than you'. Rather than investing a lot of time in trying to persuade clients about a solution, it is better to invest time in finding those good clients in the first place. Good clients will be challenging for you and they will have a higher innovation potential than you. They will persuade you to climb even higher and try even harder."

Directory

3DELUXE GRAPHICS
Wiesbaden, Germany
a.lauhoff@3deluxe.de
www.3deluxe.de

ANTOINE + MANUEL
Paris, France
www.antoineetmanuel.com
m@antoineetmanuel.com

JONATHAN BARNBROOK
London, UK
www.barnbrook.net
studio@barnbrookdesign.co.uk

BASE
Brussels, Belgium
www.basedesign.com
basebru@basedesign.com

BRANDIGLOO
Hamburg, Germany
www.brandigloo.com
info@brandigloo.com

DAG HENNING BRANDSAETER
Amsterdam, The Netherlands
www.cheapandnasty.net
dag@qua.nl

CARTLIDGE LEVENE
London, UK
www.cartlidgelevene.co.uk
ian.cartlidge@cartlidgelevene.co.uk

FRANÇOIS CHALET
Zurich, Switzerland
www.francoischalet.ch
bonjour@francoischalet.ch

JORK ANDRE DIETER
New York, USA
www.jork-andre-dieter.com
jad@jork-andre-dieter.com

DIXONBAXI
London, UK
simon@dixonbaxi.com
www.dixonbaxi.com

DOUBLE STANDARDS
Berlin, Germany
www.doublestandards.net
contact@doublestandards.net

GÜNTER EDER
Vienna, Austria
www.gued.at
mail@gued.at

ENAMEL
Tokyo, Japan
www.enamel.jp.org
factory@enamel.jp.org

FLINK
Antwerp, Belgium
www.flink.be
fanny@flink.be

FOUR23
Manchester, UK
www.four23.co.uk
warren@four23.co.uk

FULGURO
Lausanne, Switzerland
www.fulguro.ch
info@fulguro.ch

GENEVIÈVE GAUCKLER
Paris, France
www.g2works.com
genevieve@g2works.com

GREIGE
Berlin, Germany
www.greige.de
mark@greige.de

KATJA GRETZINGER
Berlin, Germany
www.mikati.net
mail@mikati.net

KLAUS HAAPANIEMI
Vicenza, Italy
www.tv-0.org
klaus@tv-0.org

FONS HICKMANN M23
Berlin, Germany
www.fonshickmann.com
fons@fonshickmann.com

HI-RES!
London, UK
www.hi-res.net
spend@hi-res.net

ITF GRAFIK DESIGN
Stuttgart, Germany
www.itfgrafikdesign.com
kahl@itfgrafikdesign.com

SEB JARNOT
Nîmes, France
www.sebjarnot.com
contact@sebjarnot.com

JUNG UND PFEFFER
Bremen, Germany
www.jungundpfeffer.de
office@jungundpfeffer.de

KASIA KORCZAK
London, UK
www.kasia-korczak.com
mail@kasia-korczak.com

PATRICK LINDSAY
Marseille, France
www.lindsay.fr
patrick@lindsay.fr

LOBO
Sao Paulo, Brazil
http://www.lobo.cx/
info@lobo.cx

LUST
The Hague, The Netherlands
www.lust.nl
lust@lust.nl

SATOSHI MATSUZAWA
Tokyo, Japan
www.salboma.com
mail@salboma.com

KENZO MINAMI
New York, USA
www.cwc-i.com
agent@cwc-i.com

MK12
Kansas City, USA
www.mk12.com
info@mk12.com

MARKUS MOSTRÖM
Stockholm, Sweden
www.mostromdesign.se
markus@mostromdesign.se

ANDY MUELLER
Los Angeles, USA
www.ohiogirl.com
info@ohiogirl.com

NEUBAU
Berlin, Germany
www.NeubauBerlin.com
Baumeister@NeubauBerlin.com

OUTPUT
Nottingham, UK
www.studio-output.com
info@studio-output.com

DIPESH PANDYA
Paris, France
dipes@address.fr

PHANTOM:RESEARCHFOUNDATION
New York, USA
www.phantomresearchfoundation.com
info@phantomresearchfoundation.com

PRECURSOR
London, UK
www.precursorstudio.com
mail@precursorstudio.com

RINZEN
Brisbane, Australia
www.rinzen.com
they@rinzen.com

SEGURA INC.
Chicago, USA
www.segura-inc.com
info@segura-inc.com

SOLAR INITIATIVE
Amsterdam, The Netherlands
www.solar.nl
initiative@solar.nl

STATE
London, UK
www.statedesign.com
info@statedesign.com

SURFACE
Frankfurt am Main, Germany
www.surface.de
info@surface.de

ANISA SUTHAYALAI
New York, USA
www.bydefault.org
info@bydefault.org

SWEDEN GRAPHICS
Stockholm, Sweden
www.swedengraphics.com
hello@swedengraphics.com

SOPHIE TOPORKOFF
Paris, France
toporkoff@address.fr

UNFOLDED
Zurich, Switzerland
www.unfolded.ch
we@unfolded.ch

VASAVA ARTWORKS
Barcelona, Spain
www.vasava.es
vasava@vasava.es

VIER5
Paris, France
www.vier5.de
kontakt@vier5.de

MARTIN WOODTLI
Zurich, Switzerland
www.woodt.li
martin@woodt.li

STEFAN YANKU
Zurich, Switzerland
www.yanku.net
stefan@yanku.net

This Gun Is for Hire
From Personal to Corporate Design Projects

Edited by Robert Klanten, Sven Ehmann, Thorsten Geiger
Text written & edited by Sophie Lovell

Editorial support Japan by Junko Hanzawa

Layout grid by Mika Mischler
Layout by Thorsten Geiger
Font: Blender by Nik Thönen / re-p

Production management by Janni Milstrey, Vinzenz Geppert

Published by Die Gestalten Verlag (dgv), Berlin • London
Printed by Jütte-Messedruck, Leipzig
Made in Germany

Bibliographic information published by
Die Deutsche Bibliothek
Die Deutsche Bibliothek lists this publication
in the Deutsche Nationalbibliografie; detailed
bibliographic data is available in the Internet at
http://dnb.ddb.de.

For more information please check out:
www.die-gestalten.de

ISBN 3-89955-054-4

Respect coypright – encourage creativity!